D1592800

Multilevel Marketing

A Lawyer Looks at Amway, Shaklee, and Other Direct Sales Organizations

Rodney K. Smith

Baker Book House
Grand Rapids, Michigan 49506

To
Danielle
my wife
without whom this book
would never have been possible

Contents

Acknowledgments   3

Introduction   5

1   The Fading American Dream   13

2   Economic Alternatives and Pitfalls   19

3   Is Multilevel Marketing the Answer?   25

4   The Saturation Objection   35

5   Not All Pyramids Are in Egypt   45

6   The Truth Is Good Enough   57

7   Cover the Down-Side Risk—And Build Profitability   73

8   A Business—Not a Tax Shelter or a Hobby   91

9   The Basics of Record Keeping   107

10   The Amway Experience   113

11   The Shaklee Opportunity   135

12   Selecting the Right Multilevel Business   151

13   Some Concluding Remarks   165

Acknowledgments

I would like to thank Dr. Jim Reed, an Amway Diamond, and Dr. Harold Berquist, a Master Coordinator in Shaklee, for their comments, criticism, discussion and encouragement. I am also grateful to Bill Joyce, my research assistant at the University of North Dakota School of Law, and John Forrester, Al Sabatini and Gerald P. Nehra, in the Legal Division of Amway Corporation, for their comments.

A number of distributors, both past and present, have contributed by example or otherwise to the writing of this book. Particularly, I am indebted to Tim and Pam Alpers, Sam and Cathy Swain, John and Libby Allred, Brian and Debbie Beach, Jim and Tonya King, Pete and Clixie Larson, Don and Marge Friel, John and Mickey Kreszwick, Glenn and Lila Prigge, Bob and Kay Fisk, Dan Henderson, and Keith and Jimmie Belknap. Since I firmly believe that distributors at all levels are the life-blood of multilevel marketing, I not only acknowledge the contribution of these distributors to the insights contained in this book, but I also commend them for their enthusiasm and effort.

Finally, I would like to thank the faculty secretaries at the University of North Dakota School of Law, Jane Clement, Rynnene Pfeifer, and Susan St. Aubyn, for their capable and seemingly tireless efforts in preparing the manuscript; and, of course, I would like to thank the editorial staff of Baker Book House who helped to make this book possible. The responsibility for any weaknesses in the content of this book ultimately is mine.

Rodney K. Smith

Introduction

I first became interested in multilevel marketing a couple of years ago when a friend of mine approached me with regard to the Amway business. My friend had recently purchased a large insurance business and was already successful in a business sense. When I learned that he was also involved in Amway, I was quite surprised, since he simply did not fit my mental image of an Amway distributor. I had the impression that Amway distributors sold soap and other products door-to-door, and I could not imagine my friend, who was college-educated and sophisticated in a business sense, selling soap. However, when he explained the Amway business, I became intrigued.

As I learned more about Amway and multilevel marketing in general, and as I watched my friend's success, I became increasingly interested in the commercial and legal implications of this type of business. I learned that there was much more to the concept of multilevel marketing than I had originally imagined. In the next couple of years, I had the opportunity to observe successful and some not-so-successful distributors for Amway, Shaklee, and other direct-sales organizations. During that period, as my rather academic interest in multilevel marketing led me through the pertinent literature available, I discovered that no one had written a book about its legal and business aspects. As a lawyer, therefore, I decided to undertake this type of analysis. This has been an exciting if somewhat time-consuming experience, and I have learned a great deal about the pros and cons of the marketing concept in action.

Perhaps my earliest and most significant discovery came when I learned that the general public's view of multilevel marketing differs greatly from reality. Many people believe that multilevel marketing is little more than a chain-letter scheme, devised to permit a few lucky (or even dishonest) people to take advantage of a large number of consumers, persuading them to part with their dollars in pursuit of an elusive dream of wealth and happiness. While this view is, in my opinion, far from the truth, particularly with regard to Amway and Shaklee, a significant portion of the fault for casting doubt on legitimate marketing businesses lies with the antics of some overzealous distributors. In an effort to convince people to join them in their businesses, some distributors have painted multilevel marketing as an easy, get-rich-quick scheme. I learned that the truth about multilevel marketing is quite different, however. I learned that a very large and growing number of participants in legitimate multilevel businesses have built extremely successful distributorships. I was also able to observe some of the common ingredients that have contributed to their success. Although some of them became successful fairly quickly, all of them worked hard on a consistent, day-in and day-out basis. In other words, in a free-enterprise sense, they earned their success by the sweat of their brows, by their labor.

I also discovered that during the past decade there has

been tremendous growth worldwide in both the number and variety of new multilevel ventures and in the number of people joining their ranks. I learned, as well, that many of the newer distributors are able to take advantage of refined business and marketing methods to build solid businesses comparable to, and sometimes even greater than, the businesses built by some of the most successful old-timers in their respective multilevel ventures. In fact, I believe it would be fair to say that I have become convinced that there really has never been a better or more propitious time than right now for someone to get involved in legitimate multilevel marketing.

With the unprecedented growth in multilevel marketing during the 1970s and into the 1980s, I have concluded that there is an immediate need for a book which would discuss all the aspects of this type of business in some depth. In fact, when I learned recently that an oil company was starting a multilevel pizza business in our community, I knew that it was time to put my thoughts on paper.

Although I tend to view legitimate multilevel marketing in a favorable light, I should point out that much of this book emphasizes how to avoid the pitfalls that some have faced in multilevel ventures. All is not always rosy. There is a way to run this type of business—and a way not to run it. Since there are distributors and specific organizations that fall into both categories, I will speak well of some and ill of others. Through it all, however, I trust that my readers will gain the information necessary to make a prudent decision as to whether or not they should get involved in a multilevel business. Furthermore, the book is also intended to give advice, in a legal and business sense, about how to operate one's business, once the determination has been made to participate.

Multilevel marketing is not for everyone, and not all who

get involved will be successful. However, there is a way to minimize one's potential risks or losses, while simultaneously maximizing one's outlook for success. Having analyzed both the successes and the failures, I feel qualified to offer some guidance along those lines.

I should note that this book is the product of my own efforts and that I have not received financial support from any multilevel business or organization in writing it. However, I have had the opportunity to discuss the substance of the contents with successful distributors and with corporate and legal officials involved in very successful multilevel enterprises. While I openly recognize my debt to many of those who have taken the time to read and comment on my findings and observations, I do not feel responsible to them, nor do I expect that they will agree with all that I have said.

I also recognize that this book may ultimately be used by some distributors as a tool to aid them in presenting the legal and business aspects of multilevel marketing to a prospect. Frankly, I am pleased by this possibility, not only because it will increase the sales of the book, but also because it may help many new and some not-so-new distributors to increase their likelihood of being successful. As such, I hope that this book will serve as yet another tool in the ever-improving and refined set of materials available to help a hard-working distributor to build a solid business organization.

I would like to make a final point. As an attorney, my advice is generally conservative. I am not only concerned with presenting the potential for success in the framework of multilevel marketing, but I am also concerned that those who participate keep their potential losses to a minimum. Therefore, I fully expect that those involved in multilevel marketing who recommend that the new distributor should load up on inventory, tools, or other business aids preparatory to entering the business will frown on the contents of much of my book. If, however, I can encourage them to think about and respond to the points raised in opposition to their philosophy of large initial expenditures by a new distributor, I will view my book as a further success. In this light, I would hope that readers would ask the questions I raise of any sponsor who would have them put a lot of up-front money into their business—and I pray that they will listen closely and carefully to their sponsor's reply.

Having dealt with the reasons for the writing of this book, I would like to conclude this introduction by summarizing the basic content of each of the chapters that will follow. This summary should help guide the reader who is looking for information related to a specific topic or problem, and it will also give the reader a feel for what will follow.

In the first chapter, "The Fading American Dream," I briefly examine the ongoing economic pressures faced by Americans in the eighties. In an era when salary increases consistently lag behind cost-of-living figures, more and more people are trying to alleviate their feelings of economic helplessness by seeking sources of additional income.

In "Economic Alternatives and Pitfalls" (chapter 2), I examine why two economic options—owning a small independent business or franchising—may not be the answer for some individuals. Both of these forms of entrepreneurship generally require a sizable investment for start-up costs and initial operating costs. In the case of franchising, there are low-cost opportunities, but generally such businesses lack a proven track record and thereby constitute a higher business risk.

"Is Multilevel Marketing the Answer?" (chapter 3) looks into the broad up-side potential of multilevel marketing, as well as the negative factors. By examining both sides of the story, a reader is better able to decide if this particular type of venture is the right one for him or her.

In "The Saturation Objection" (chapter 4), I discuss a number of reasons why I believe there is little danger of market saturation for the product line of a legitimate multilevel organization such as Amway or Shaklee. Furthermore, I point out that there is unlikely to be a shortage of potential distributors for such products in the foreseeable future.

In "Not All Pyramids Are in Egypt" (chapter 5), I explain the differences between legitimate multilevel marketing and the pyramid or chain-letter schemes which plagued this country in the fifties and sixties (and which still occasionally put in an unwelcome appearance today). In examining, as a legal matter, what constitutes an illegal pyramid, I show why reputable businesses do not fall into this category.

In "The Truth Is Good Enough" (chapter 6), I do battle, as both a legal and practical consideration, with those who feel compelled to embellish the truth when presenting a multilevel opportunity. Legal action may be brought against individuals who intentionally or even negligently misrepresent their organization's sales program or compensation plan, or who overstate the income made by an average distributor in that business. Furthermore, reputable multilevel organizations such as Amway or Shaklee terminate distributors who repeatedly indulge in such exaggeration. I also point out that it is foolish and impractical to misrepresent the facts concerning a particular business. The best prospects will soon uncover the truth and may therefore become disenchanted with the operation because they believe they were deceived.

"Cover the Down-Side Risk—And Build Profitability" (chapter 7) discusses inventory loading (the requirement that a new distributor buy a large amount of inventory to get started or continue in the business, thus incurring a significant debt). Inventory loading and incurrence of debt for other unnecessary items are counterproductive and can stymie the efforts of a new distributor to build a profitable business. Initial unexpected economic strain can cause a distributor to become bitter about the very idea of the new business. This is particularly unfortunate since often a disillusioned distributor might have made a success of the venture if he or she had been given more time and encouragement.

"A Business—Not a Tax Shelter or a Hobby" (chapter 8) points out that legitimate multilevel businesses should be operated primarily for the purpose of making money—not solely as a tax shelter or for the alleged tax benefits. Like most businesses, multilevel marketing offers tax deductions for *legitimate* business expenses. While I summarize some of the tax aspects of operating a multilevel business, I emphasize the need for strict compliance with existing tax law, as both a moral and legal matter.

In "The Basics of Record Keeping" (chapter 9), I outline a few techniques and devices which not only facilitate the operation of any business, but will help satisfy the IRS requirement for documentation of tax-deductible expenses.

Chapters 10 and 11, respectively, deal with "The Amway Experience" and "The Shaklee Opportunity." While these chapters depict some of the unique aspects of each of these business ventures, the emphasis is on their similarities, because it is those common features that illustrate why both organizations can provide attractive business opportunities.

In these chapters, I briefly summarize how the Amway and Shaklee businesses developed and what they are doing to ensure significant growth in the future, both at the corporate level and among the ranks of distributors. While I believe the facts given are helpful to a would-be distributor, I have refrained from indicating my preference between the two. I firmly believe that they are both great opportunities, and one or the other may have more appeal to particular individuals.

In "Selecting the Right Multilevel Business" (chapter 12), I essentially turn from the Amway and Shaklee businesses to discuss other multilevel opportunities. Although I offer some advice as to what to look for in evaluating these new businesses, I do not discuss them individually.

In chapter 13, "Some Concluding Remarks," I summarize my conclusions and offer some final comments about the future of multilevel marketing.

This book is more than an analysis of an attractive business opportunity. I hope that it is also about how legitimate multilevel marketing, an integral part of our free-enterprise system, can still provide people with the opportunity to make their economic dreams come true through honest, consistent, and confident toil. May the reading of this book be an interesting and provocative introduction to the business for a new or potential distributor and a reaffirmation and welcome reminder of what multilevel marketing is all about for the not-so-new distributor.

1

The Fading American Dream

Is multilevel marketing for "everyone," as an overly exuberant distributor might claim? Or is it for "no one," in the words of many an uninformed detractor?

Obviously, neither pat reply is particularly helpful in explaining the current popularity of this unique form of free enterprise—or in guiding the decision-making process of someone contemplating becoming involved in such a business.

The major motivation for entering and succeeding in a multilevel business is perceived economic need. Simply stated, people are not making enough money to satisfy their desire for economic improvement. As long as people desire additional income to attain a preconceived standard of living, and as long as multilevel businesses are a means of meeting those material objectives, this type of economic opportunity will appeal to a significant number of people.

I recently asked a group of young people what their greatest fear was. I was startled by the predominant answer: They were afraid of never being able to own their own home as their parents had. As I reflected on their response, it became clear that their apprehension was

13

generally well-founded. At the time, I was living in California, where even the most inexpensive tract home costs nearly $100,000. With the customary down payment and prevailing interest rates, monthly payments on such a home usually exceed $1,000.

Many young people in America feel cheated today. Economic developments in the last two decades, with inflation continually rearing its ugly head, place home ownership out of reach for many. Young people, it seems, no longer have the opportunity to pursue the American Dream as previous generations did.

As a teenager, I believed that one day I would be able to afford to own my own home and enjoy the other material aspects of "the good life." Back then, the house that today costs $100,000 could have been purchased for less than $20,000, with monthly payments that barely reached $200. At that time I did not have to worry about not being able to purchase a home when the time came; nearly everyone could afford to do so. If I worked hard and saved my money, only the sky would be the limit. In fact, my assumptions were correct. Most of my generation have been able to enjoy the basic blessing of the American Dream, although the toil required to attain this economic level may have exceeded earlier expectations.

But today it is different. With each jump in inflation in the last twenty years, there has been a corresponding decline in the material expectations of young Americans. With hard work, the previous generation may have been able to reach their economic goals, including home ownership. However, for those now entering the marketplace, perseverance no longer seems to provide adequate assurance that anyone can achieve the dream of owning a home. Although wages tend to increase to reflect the inflationary spiral, real income always lags behind cost-of-living increases—and nowhere is this more evident than in the housing area.

A recent Associated Press article, originating in Washington, D.C., reported that the longer-term outlook for home ownership is a sobering one, plagued by such far-flung problems as the apparent inability of government to trim the record budget deficits and the unlikelihood that adults who grew out of the "baby boom" will be able to save very much of their income.

The article went on to note that the percentage of American homes that are owned or are being bought by their occupants had declined to 64.8 percent—after rising, even through recessions, since the 1940s. The affordability gap—the difference between what a typical first-time buyer might be able to pay for a house and the actual price of available housing—had widened to about $20,000 since it first showed up in 1979. The article concluded that the most important recommendation to end the plight of the would-be homeowner is for the government to trim its budget deficits. Unfortunately, the prospective buyer of a first home can take little solace in this recommendation, not only because the federal budget is out of an individual's direct control, but also because of the disheartening track record of the government in failing to conquer deficit spending. Therefore, it is no wonder that so many people find their hopes for home ownership, or for that matter, any economic improvement, little more than an empty dream. There seems to be no happy ending to the unfolding drama of this economic nightmare.

To overcome this depressing state of affairs, with a sometimes wavering belief in free enterprise, many couples have broken the once-traditional structure of family life, in which the husband worked and the wife stayed home with the children. For many, the two-income family is a matter of choice. For others, it is a matter of economic survival. Ann Landers recently highlighted this trend in an article which appeared in the November 16, 1982, issue of *Family Circle:*

> Another dramatic change in family life is the phenomenon of the working wife. In the past 20 years the number of women who have joined the work force has doubled. The most recent survey available (1980) pegs the figure at close to 24 million. This means more than half the married women in the United States are employed outside the home.
>
> While college-educated wives without children usually work because they want to, the vast majority of women with children under 12 years of age admit frankly that they would much rather stay home. Their reason for taking jobs is that the family can't make it financially on one paycheck. The woman who is forced to leave her kids in a day-care center or with a baby-sitter is often deeply resentful, and such feelings don't help an already ailing marriage.

Many husbands and wives have responded realistically to what they consider to be economic reality—both must work during the most productive years of their lives to pay their bills and to reap some of the economic benefits that accrue to the two-income family. With housing often beyond the reach of a family with a single breadwinner, it may be within the reach of that same family if both spouses work. Similarly, college education and other benefits may be affordable for their children if both parents work, whereas these same items would be difficult to finance with only one income.

The economic advantage gained when both spouses work is not without problems. On the one hand, a spouse may have to work when he or she would prefer to stay home. On the other hand, both partners may sincerely desire to work but face the option of foregoing or postponing a family or of encountering the additional strain of raising a family with the attendant financial and emotional costs of prolonged child care. Additional strains are often put on parental and spousal relationships as well. The point here is not to take sides in regard to these volatile and very personal issues. Rather, it should be emphasized that current economic conditions often require making difficult choices, and such circumstances sometimes eliminate the opportunity for choice in certain areas of life.

Even when both spouses are working, economic improvement is not reached without difficulties. Income does not always meet outflow. Salaries may not keep pace with inflation and income-tax bracketing. Jobs, when available (over one-third of all Americans receive direct government aid), often seem to be unsatisfactory. Advancement based on merit and productivity has been replaced by notions such as seniority and tenure. Even the bureaucracies typical of most private enterprises appear to be ruled as much by office politics as by actual accomplishment. The essence of free enterprise—that individuals are rewarded according to their personal productivity—no longer seems to hold a central position in the national and international marketplace.

Although I have been discussing primarily the financial plight of younger couples, no age or demographic group on our national scene seems to be immune to economic insecurity. For middle-aged and middle-income Americans, the rising cost of education and related spiraling expenses involved in raising children have together contributed to a heightened sense of economic frustration. According to a recent estimate, the cost of raising a child rose from $68,232 in 1980 to $80,926 in 1982. These figures, like those dealing with the purchase of a home, are staggering and with certainty affect the quality of family life.

Finally, older Americans find themselves in an even more precarious position. They have discovered that social security and other pension plans rarely provide the freedom and economic security that they had hoped to attain upon retirement. Furthermore, their job opportunities are limited.

Confronted with mounting economic pressure, many people, both young and old, have had to work at a frantic pace just to maintain a modest lifestyle. This stark economic reality has produced despair and literally dashed the dreams of many. To make matters worse, when inflation and recession joined hands in the late 1970s and early 1980s, many people had to worry not only about maintaining or enhancing their quality of life, but about keeping their jobs. As employees, their future became increasingly unclear. As a result, many have considered or actually started a business of their own, as we shall see in the next chapter.

2

Economic Alternatives and Pitfalls

Entry into the business world is neither easy nor without risk. The difficult conditions that have made entrepreneurship an alluring option and almost a necessity for many people have also contributed to an increase in the number of filings in bankruptcy courts. In 1979, there were 226,476 filings for bankruptcy; in 1980, 360,957; in 1981, 519,083. Changes in bankruptcy laws account for part of this accelerated trend, but the economic climate of those years also played an important role. Each bankruptcy represents economic failure and intense emotional trauma for all concerned. A bankruptcy usually represents the dashing to pieces of someone's dream. Although most people assume that hard work ensures success in the business world, such an assumption has proven untrue. The many risks attending entry into business can be counteracted by hard work and long hours, but there are some factors that are simply beyond the control of even the most conscientious businessperson.

The massive economic and emotional risks related to starting up almost any kind of business are often accentuated by fluctuations in the marketplace. For example, I had two close friends who got involved in a farming business. Both, along with their families, worked as hard as could humanly be expected, but they failed, ending up in a bankruptcy which dissolved not only their business but ultimately their friendship. The market simply refused to cooperate—the price paid for their products went down, while their operating costs rose. Two of the finest families I have known have suffered greatly as a result of uncontrollable factors on the national economic scene.

Starting a new business requires much advance planning and organizational skill. A location must be obtained and made operational. Employees must be hired and trained. Consumers must be encouraged to purchase the product or service offered. Books and records must be maintained. The list of administrative and maintenance concerns is almost endless.

Planning and organization, however, are just the beginning. Operating a business requires daily, sometimes hourly, attention. With only twenty-four hours in a day, time management becomes a critical factor in the life of a person who takes on a new business. Time creates its own form of risk. It takes time for almost any type of new business to develop—to move from the red to the black and become a profitable enterprise. The new businessperson is confronted with the same clock demands we all face, but the new business often seems to demand more attention than the allotted hours permit. No new business can linger indefinitely in the red as a money-losing venture; it must become profitable rather quickly, since start-up capital for small businesses is usually limited in amount and accessibility.

These points can be illustrated by returning to the example of my friends who started a new farming operation. Initially, one of them had to work full-time in another business to make enough money to service the start-up loans and to keep the business operating while it was in its nonprofitable stage. Later, the second principal also had to obtain full-time employment away from the new business. The new venture inevitably began to suffer from inattention. Both of my friends knew that the business would be successful if they could remain operational until the market changed for the better, as it ultimately did. However, the prevailing market factors and the concurrent inattention ultimately led to a storm that could not be weathered. Time, coupled with market conditions, led to an economic failure and strained personal relationships.

Most persons who go into business for themselves take on such risks, but there are ways of limiting them. One way is to purchase a franchise with a proven track record. In an article that appeared in the September 13, 1982, issue of *Forbes* magazine, Thomas P. Murphy explained why franchising is a common choice for Americans who seek a business to operate. He noted that over 500,000 Americans have purchased franchises because: "Instead of the risk and anguish of venturing out on your own, a sound franchisor offers a proven product, a refined business system, training, advertising, and most importantly, a knowledge of what works and what doesn't."

Since a healthy franchised business opportunity helps to minimize many risks, one might ask why anyone would go into business without the aid of a proven franchise. The answer to this question can be summarized in one word: *cost.* To start a franchised operation, in addition to the usual start-up costs related to developing a new business enterprise (such as the acquisition of property and equipment), the franchisee (the party purchasing the franchise) must pay the franchisor a substantial fee. Unfortunately, people who are looking for a way out of economic difficulties rarely have the money necessary to purchase a franchise.

By way of illustration, an article in the June 7, 1982, issue of *Business Week* referred to the ownership of a major franchise as a "rich man's dream." Land and building costs for one of the big-name fast-food chains averaged around $350,000 in 1981—with additional working capital requirements of at least $300,000. Clearly, there are few people who can afford such a large capital investment, and those with limited tangible assets of their own might have difficulty in obtaining a loan to cover these start-up costs.

Furthermore, major franchisors are increasingly opening company-owned establishments (or selling franchises only to those who already own a successful outlet). Since the risk of opening a new facility has been somewhat minimized, once the name has been established, the parent company may understandably wish to avoid sharing the profits with a middleman.

There are, of course, franchise opportunities available at minimal investment costs, some as low as $20,000. However, a lower cost may signify a higher risk factor. Dance studios, fitness centers, or doughnut shops, for example, may take longer to establish on a profitable basis, even when the company name is recognized by the general public. Specialized facilities may require intensive research by the franchisee into choice of location, existing competition, and even whether the business would provide a service or product reflecting the needs of the local population.

Finally, even where the needed capital is available, the franchisee can expect to spend considerable time in overseeing the fledgling business, especially in the early stages. He or she may find it necessary to leave a regular job to do so. If the franchise fails, or the owner otherwise wishes to return to that job, he or she may find that option unavailable, or at the very least may have sacrificed seniority and chances for advancement.

Facing these sobering economic facts of life, some individuals and couples are willing to consider multilevel marketing as a viable business venture and a way out of their economic dilemma. I can tell you right now that it is no panacea—not everyone who gets involved in multilevel selling succeeds, but many do so with minimized risks. The next chapter concerns the general benefits and burdens (there are some!) of the multilevel business opportunity.

3

Is Multilevel Marketing the Answer?

In a legitimate multilevel marketing arrangement, distributors engage in both direct selling and in sponsoring new distributors for the business, thereby building a sales organization. When a new distributor is recruited, his or her sponsor receives a percentage override or bonus, based on that new distributor's sales volume. In any reputable multimarketing business, it must be emphasized, new distributors will generally make more money from their own individual and group sales volume than do the sponsors. Thus, if the new distributors' volume (including that of the sales group) increases to a point beyond that of their respective sponsors, they should make more money from the business than the sponsors, unless the sponsors maintain an equivalent volume of sales of their own.

In this sense, a multilevel business is based on classic free enterprise, since compensation is directly related to productivity. Typically, a distributor earns a decreasing percentage of sales by his or her "downline" (e.g., 5 percent for first level, 2 percent for second level, 1 percent for third level, and so on). This commission, override, or bonus is *in addition* to the commission received for the distributor's own personal sales. Compensation varies from business to business, but the principle is always the same—a distributor is compensated for both personal sales and "downline" sales. Thus, there is an ever-present desire to sell, as well as to build a sales organization.

In many respects, the legitimate multilevel business opportunity resembles a franchise, in that there are available established products, a sound administrative procedure, sales training, and advertising facilities. Multilevel marketing offers many of these features, but does not require a substantial up-front expense as does a franchise.

Multilevel marketing in the framework of a reputable organization can provide the following:

1. A proven product that is consumed on a repeated basis. For example, Amway and Shaklee sell cleaning products and nutritional needs which are consumed and thus repurchased in a regular cycle.
2. A refined business system and established administrative procedure. Multilevel businesses offer a viable compensation plan and materials explaining how the system works.
3. Built-in training. The most successful distributors maximize their own success by recruiting new distributors and training them to be successful, too.
4. Advertising arrangements. Although some parent companies limit their national advertising campaigns to keep product costs low, most do provide their distributors with advertising materials which are adapted to the multilevel marketing concept.
5. Knowledge of what works. Again, a distributor maintains a high success level by recruiting other distributors with

whom to share the knowledge of previously successful selling techniques.

As already noted, the major difference between a sound franchise and a legitimate multimarketing business is the significantly reduced cost of the latter, since financial investment should be minimal. This is in stark contrast to the substantial start-up fees required for purchasing a franchise.

For a person lacking extensive economic resources and/or business training and experience, multilevel marketing may offer the best business opportunity in the 1980s. Additionally, it should be noted that a multilevel business can (and generally should be) run without any major operational expense, thereby posing no possible threat of bankruptcy for the new distributor. Moreover, economic risk can be controlled without adversely affecting the productive potential of the business. Any incipient risks are of a noneconomic nature.

One significant consideration is the loss of time. Anyone who intends to be successful in a multilevel marketing endeavor must be willing to expend a substantial number of hours in the venture. Do not be misled by any claim that—with only a few hours per week—you can build a thriving, profitable business. No successful distributorship can succeed without hard work, sometimes extending over unusual hours. Generally, fifteen to twenty hours weekly are required to achieve even moderate success. Although there is some flexibility in the time scheduling, this business simply will not run itself. Many new distributors delude themselves into believing that if they just sponsor three or four good "downline" distributors, these recruits will do all the work, and they themselves can "retire." A multilevel business does not work this way. Once a distributor has a few first-level distributors, the time commitment is even more demanding. First of all, the initial distributor must continue to train and encourage his immediate "downline," and must also work with those at lower levels. Second, since there is a substantial turnover rate for lower-level distributors, particularly when they are inadequately trained, the original recruiter must persist in sponsoring at the first level, as well as service some retail customers. If a distributor ceases to sponsor, it is likely that people he or she sponsored in the program will follow suit. With ongoing responsibility for contacting potential distributors, training the "downline," and handling some retail orders, twenty hours can easily be consumed in one week.

It should be noted, however, that even though there are substantial time demands, the hourly expenditure does not (*and should not*) require that a distributor give up his or her existing employment. (Many achieve so high a success rate that they are eventually able to leave their primary occupation.) One of the most attractive features of a multilevel business is that it can be operated on a part-time basis. With most business meetings held during the evening or on a one-to-one basis at a mutually acceptable time, there are usually few scheduling conflicts between one's multimarketing efforts and a regular job. The necessary time expenditure can, however, negatively influence performance in one's employed capacity. If your attention is diverted to your marketing activities during regular working hours, or if you pressure fellow workers too hard to get involved in that extracurricular venture, problems can easily arise.

By properly allocating your time and energy and making the important distinction between your primary occupation and your marketing distributorship, this pitfall can be avoided. In fact, in my observation of the regular work performance of individuals participating in the two income-producing activities, I have noted that performance in both may improve. Success in marketing/selling requires a positive approach in dealing with others, an attitude which carries over into other relationships, including those in a regular job.

Unlike most other economic ventures, a multilevel business allows a person to work at his or her own pace—with the already noted warning that it is difficult to build a successful distributorship without investing a significant amount of time on a regular basis. It should be noted that consistency is critical. In my observation, successful distributors, week after week, regularly invest time and effort in their business. Consistency is often as important as the actual number of hours logged.

Although market fluctuations and the general economy can adversely affect any business, multilevel organizations such as Amway and Shaklee have essentially evidenced substantial and consistent growth since their inception. Even if there were an economic downturn which were to affect multilevel sales, the worst that could probably happen to a distributor is the loss of all or part of his or her marketing organization. Again, since both investment (other than time) and debt can be limited, losses can always be kept to a minimum.

It may sound too good to be true to learn that the only conventional risk involved in multilevel marketing is the loss of one's time. However, there is another phenomenon that seems to affect this type of business in a unique way. I will refer to that concept as the risk of status or the status objection.

Since people do not normally approach distributors and

request the opportunity to get involved in a given business, the distributors themselves must contact friends and acquaintances to "sell" them the same type of opportunity. Contacting associates and even close friends to invite them to a presentation meeting can be difficult and awkward. It takes a special kind of fortitude to recruit a new distributor or even sell a product under those circumstances.

While I do not personally know of anyone who has actually lost a friend after inviting him or her to a distributorship meeting, I am aware that some distributors have felt rebuffed while approaching someone for that purpose. More significantly, however, I know people who have felt a lapse of status in the eyes of others. Most novice distributors and even some not-so-new ones wonder about what their involvement in Amway, Shaklee, or other such organized sales programs will mean to their friends and neighbors. After all, people do not generally set lifetime goals related to selling cleaning supplies or vitamins—they more likely dream of being actors, doctors, or lawyers! Normally, at least in the beginning, even the most enthusiastic distributor does not brag about selling soap.

In a somewhat similar sense, many people have an aversion to the very idea of such a business venture, because they do not relish the concept of being a salesperson. Some direct selling is always necessary, even though most successful distributors spend the vast majority of their time in sponsoring and training new recruits. Despite my view that everyone is a salesperson in some sense (for example, as a college professor, I sell my knowledge and my service as a teacher), there is something that many consider demeaning about selling household, nutritional, or related products.

The reason Amway, Shaklee, and similar organizations deal primarily with this type of item is actually quite simple. For a multilevel business to grow on a consistent basis, it must engender regular and recurrent sales (preferably monthly). Cleaning products, vitamins, and the like are most conducive to repetitive sales, since they are generally consumed on a consistent schedule. Additionally, by their choice of such goods, Amway and Shaklee can open the doors of opportunity to people in all backgrounds. Since virtually anyone can be trained to sell them, attention can be directed to developing a solid sales program.

In my current employment as a law professor, I have certain credentials (after twenty-one years in school), and this documentation, so to speak, has given me a certain status. To my students, I am Professor Smith; to my clients, I am Rodney K. Smith, attorney. I have earned this status (and perhaps even deserved it). In a multilevel business, academic credentials and other status symbols make little difference in the success levels attained. In fact, they may even get in the way of success, which in this instance is based solely on performance and productivity. This is disturbing, perhaps, to a person who has come to rely on his or her résumé, rather than on individual capacity to produce tangible results.

The general irrelevance of credentials—and the perceived belief that participation in a multilevel distributorship may actually reduce one's status in the eyes of others—causes many people to bypass this economic opportunity. While other risks are low, the potential loss of status may be considered overwhelming.

This assumed loss of stature creates a major factor to be considered when contemplating involvement in a legitimate multilevel sales program. While there is nothing illegal, immoral, or unethical about this type of business, the very nature of the activity makes some people uneasy.

Frankly, I believe that such objections are unwarranted and misdirected. In our contemporary world, we have become overly status-conscious. As more and more jobs require specialized training, degrees and other credentials have become the necessary tickets for entering certain new occupations. This is understandable and perhaps necessary in a highly technical society. However, multilevel marketing, while requiring some training, does not rely on specific entry-level qualifications. It is pure free enterprise, which generally rewards a person strictly in accordance with his or her productive efforts.

There is one sense in which the status objection may be somewhat justified, however. Some overzealous distributors have misrepresented the business arrangements or have used deceit in order to draw an audience receptive to their sales pitch. Major multilevel marketing organizations such as Amway and Shaklee try to enforce their strict codes of ethics in order to prevent exaggeration and deceit, although such vigilance has not been able to eliminate them entirely. Occasional unethical practices have, in turn, caused many a person to view multilevel market itself as suspect. This is unfortunate and unfair, and no one benefits from this attitude.

As it is with those who preach the gospel, I would suggest that it is improvident to confuse the minister with the message. A minister—or by analogy, an overeager distributor—may on occasion indulge in questionable behavior, although that does not make the entire message improper. Nevertheless, it is not uncommon to see someone "turned off" to a multilevel business opportunity simply because of the manner in which it was presented, rather than the actual substance of the compensation arrangements. As will be pointed out later, in the case of multilevel marketing, the truth is always the most moral and practical policy.

There is a final risk inherent in multilevel marketing, just as it is in any business: the chance of failure. Based on a recent survey, only 40 percent of Amway's distributors energetically pursue their business possibilities. Among those, only about 15 percent actively sponsor other distributors. Thus, less than one out of every four Amway distributors is really involved in building a sales organization. This is also true of Shaklee and similar legitimate multilevel ventures.

However, the percentages cited do not actually represent a high rate of business failures. Many who sign up as Amway or Shaklee distributors do so with little intention of developing a thriving business. They may have been attracted merely by the products offered and the opportunity to buy them at the distributor's price rather than the suggested retail price. Such participants may have little interest in sponsoring others, although on occasion they may do so. To classify these persons as business failures would be a mistake. However, it is possible for a person to become a distributor with full intention of developing a good business and yet fail to do so. Failure may result from a variety of circumstances, among which may be lack of persistence, inattention to details, poor presentation of the products, or for any of a variety of other reasons. Again, the risk of failure in the monetary sense is minimal, since the financial investment is so very little.

For people who can disregard the status factor and realistically accept the emotional pain of failure, there may be no more appealing road to economic well-being than multilevel marketing for a reputable organization. For some people whose material needs are apparently being priced out of the market, this type of business venture can provide the ability to meet their real or perceived requirements. Whether as a supplement to a regular job or as a full-time activity, it is not unusual for multilevel marketing to add $1,000 monthly to the family income. The greatest challenge for many is merely the stamina to accept a "no" from a potential customer or sponsoring recruit.

4

The Saturation Objection

One of the major objections raised by the critics of multilevel selling arrangements is that the potential market is already saturated. These detractors allege that distributors are no longer likely to recruit other new selling agents because recruitment of additional distributors must ultimately collapse when those already recruited have so saturated an area as to render it virtually impossible to recruit other distributors or dealers. Actually, those who assert that the market is saturated make two somewhat independent claims: (1) that there is no one left to be sponsored, because everyone interested in a given market is already involved; and (2) that there are no customers left to purchase the product in that selling area. To analyze these issues, I will concentrate on the experience of Amway and Shaklee. Since they are the largest multilevel marketing enterprises, they would conceivably face saturation, if the problem does, in fact, exist.

At least during the foreseeable future, these objections are not well founded. The understanding of why saturation is not a serious objection can best be gleaned from an examination of some recent legal developments.

In 1975, a complaint was filed before the Federal Trade

Commission against Amway Corporation, alleging that distributors in Amway "are not long likely to recruit other distributors . . . or to profit from sales to other distributors at lower functional levels. . . ." In support of these allegations, the complainants asserted that Amway's recruitment plan must ultimately collapse "when the number of potentially available persons who can be recruited to serve a particular area is exhausted. . . ." They also argued: "The greater the number of levels of distribution the more inefficient the Amway distribution system becomes, and the less profitable it is likely to be at lower levels." Essentially, the complainants alleged that Amway was destined to fall apart when the market became saturated with the product and projected distributors. In conclusion, therefore, they asserted that when the market became so saturated, there would no longer be an opportunity for distributors at lower levels to either sponsor new recruits or sell additional product.

Of course, although Amway Corporation refused to concede this point, the government lawyers on the other side would not relent. Both parties then began to prepare for litigation by accumulating evidence to be produced in conjunction with a proceeding before an independent administrative law judge.

The government officials who drafted the complaint against Amway produced a number of witnesses who testified of their difficulty in sponsoring new distributors in their particular areas of the country. On the other hand, empirical evidence presented by Amway proved that the opportunity to sponsor new distributors in all those areas continued unabated.

For example, a government witness testified that Baton Rouge, Louisiana, was saturated with the Amway operation. Amway countered by offering actual testimony to the effect that distributors in Baton Rouge increased from 332 in 1975 to 546 in 1976. This represented an increase in new distributorships of over 64 percent during the very year it was claimed that the area was glutted. The government countered by claiming that Charlotte, North Carolina, was similarly saturated. Amway, in turn, responded that during the year in question (from 1975 to 1976) distributorships in Charlotte increased from 688 to 1,014, an increase of over 47 percent. The government made similar assertions with regard to Conway, South Carolina; certain counties in Florida; Dallas/Fort Worth, Texas; and Kalamazoo, Michigan. In every case, Amway countered with actual data showing that large numbers of new distributors were sponsored into the business during the period in question. After hearing this testimony the judge noted on the record, as a finding of fact, that "witnesses whom I have heard and find credible were called by respondents [Amway] and testified that in several of these areas they had no difficulty sponsoring new distributors during the relevant time." It is not surprising, therefore, that the judge concluded that "the facts in this record do not show that Amway distributors in any market were unable to recruit new distributors or to sell Amway projects because of any inherent defect in the Amway Sales and Marketing Plan." The judge went on to note in his decision that he believed "the reason for their failure [to sponsor] was more accurately described by a marketing expert who testified about this subject (Patty, Tr. 3109): 'I think generally speaking when a salesman tells you that a market is saturated, he has become discouraged for some reason, usually he is simply not making the sales effort that is required. . . .'"

Interestingly, in support of his conclusions, the judge also made the following observation, based on the hearing and his review of literally thousands of pages of testimony: "It is relatively unlikely that the available supply of potential Amway distributors will be exhausted in any particular area."

Citing specific testimony, the judge commented that Amway is predominantly a part-time activity, to which former distributors sometime returned. He also observed that although only one-fourth of the distributors actually engage in sponsoring, there had been no decline in this activity during the previous five or six years. Relevant testimony indicated that Amway's sales growth was virtually uninterrupted during the period in question, both nationally and state by state. Likewise, the Amway distributors' average monthly income had also been increasing.

Whatever theoretical problems saturation may pose, it apparently has been proven to carry little weight on the practical level.

Since the FTC action against Amway, the facts have been even more startling. Estimated yearly sales at retail for Amway have grown from about $250,000,000 in 1975 (the date that the saturation charge was brought against Amway) to $1.13 billion in 1983—an increase of over 400 percent. Additionally, and perhaps more significantly in terms of income potential, the number of distributors who have entered the most lucrative compensation levels in Amway has also evidenced substantial growth. For example, in 1982 alone, over 5,000 distributors moved up to higher compensation levels at the direct level and above. (To qualify as a Direct, a distributor must have actual sales of approximately $13,000 or more each month.) It is not unusual for a new Direct to make $1,000 or more per month in gross income, before being adjusted for tax purposes, and many of the higher "pins" (compensation levels) represent incomes of $100,000 or more per year. To further illustrate that there is room at the very top, there were thirteen Crown Direct distributors for Amway in 1983. This is the highest level in Amway, and although I do not have the figures on their annual incomes, I am confident that they are well into hundreds of thousands of dollars. All of these Crown Directs reached that level in 1977 or later, and two of these distributors did not even sign up in Amway until 1977. Another joined in 1976 and still another in 1974. Since the government brought its action against Amway in 1975, there has been an enormous growth in the business at all levels, and recent activity would indicate no immediate saturation difficulty whatsoever.

The story has been essentially the same for Shaklee, although this organization was not subject to a similar legal action. Robert L. Shook in his book, *The Shaklee Story*, made the following observation:

> *Financial World* has stated that during the 1970s Shaklee was the number two company on the New York Stock Exchange in terms of sales potential. This statement was based on Shaklee's incredible gain in sales, from $20 million in 1970 to $314 million in 1979. The following year, sales volume was $411 million, an amazing increase of 31 percent. In 1981 sales moved still higher, toward the half billion mark.

After reviewing the performance potential of Shaklee, in their independent company analysis of May 16, 1981, the investment firm of Salomon Brothers concluded: "If Shaklee were particularly successful in planning its field operations it could probably achieve 15–20% growth a year in its sales force with an impressive 20–25% earnings growth a year. . . ." As to the potential for sponsorship, Salomon Brothers added that "Shaklee's sales leader force could grow 10%–15% a year during the next several years from what is a very low base of 10,100 in direct selling."

As Shaklee experiences sales growth, its distributors, as those in Amway, receive added compensation. Thus, while Shaklee's sales grew from $275,000,000 in 1978 to $411,000,000 in 1980, the volume of incentives (bonuses or compensation) paid to distributors also grew from $116,000,000 in 1978 to $171,500,000 in 1980, a growth of nearly 50 percent in just two years.

As the recent phenomenal growth of Amway and Shaklee amply illustrates, there are no indications that such legitimate multilevel operations face significant market saturation. A careful examination of their operations reveals several reasons for this promising outlook. First, both Amway and Shaklee make continual adjustments in their product lines to respond to changing demands in the marketplace. They also continue to price their products competitively. Additionally, neither Amway nor Shaklee, the two giants of multilevel marketing, control enough of their respective markets to pose a serious threat to future sales expansion. On a regular basis, Amway has expanded its line from basic home-care products into the realm of personal care, nutrition, housewares—and even a mail order or personal shoppers' catalog service. Furthermore, in each of these areas, Amway has continued to add new products. By 1983, Amway offered some 350 different items, excluding those sold through its catalog service. These new products range from one of the highest-rated burglary alarms on the market to cosmetics and jewelry.

Shaklee, on the other hand, has cut its overall product offerings in the past few years, in an effort to keep prices down through consolidation of its production capacity. Shaklee's line continues to include nutritional items, household products, and various personal items. According to the Salomon Brothers report, "growth in vitamins is expected to equal 10%–15% annually in dollar sales . . . making vitamins one of the more attractive personal needs categories in terms of unit growth." Shaklee continues to lead in research and development in the vitamin and nutrition area. Shaklee, like Amway, has made advances in the growing and lucrative snack-food business, a multi-billion dollar business in this country alone.

To paint an even rosier picture for the future, both Amway and Shaklee have moved into international markets. There is also significant room for growth in the United States, even in the areas already serviced by Amway and Shaklee. For example, collectively, Amway and Shaklee have much less than 5% of the household-products market, and they have substantial room for growth, in the nutrition area. The prospect for growth in sponsorship of new distributors is equally promising for the following reasons:

1. The population of the country continues to grow.

2. The opportunity for long-distance sponsoring in other domestic and international areas has expanded. Some sales groups even make a computer printout or similar information available to new distributors, indicating time and place of distributor meetings in other cities. A distributor can send a contract to such a meeting and personally sponsor others into the business from afar. Internationally, the corporation will often support distributors in their efforts to sponsor at a distance.

3. Many contacts who have previously shown disinter-

est in the compensation plan subsequently get involved in the business after a second look. This new enthusiasm may be based on a change in their personal affairs or on a difference in the personality and presentation method of the recruiter.

4. The growth potential is indirectly affected by the large number of distributors who drop out of Amway each year, often as many as 50 percent of the existing distributors. (Since most direct-sales businesses have an annual drop-out rate of nearly 100 percent, this figure is actually low.) As many as 75 percent of the new distributors in Amway fail to renew after their first year. However, even of those distributors who stay, only about 25 percent actively work at sponsoring other distributors. Many are obviously content just to purchase the products at a discount, perhaps engaging in a little selling, but without sponsoring. Shaklee, on the other hand, does not have corresponding drop-out figures, because there is no requirement for renewal of a distributorship each year, as is the case with Amway. However, it is clear that only a very small percentage of the people signed up in Shaklee actively engage in sponsoring. This drop-out rate, coupled with the rate of inactivity in terms of sponsorship, has two implications for the present discussion. First, it illustrates that it is somewhat difficult to retain active distributors. Second, despite the drop-out rate, both Amway and Shaklee have experienced phenomenal growth in their sales force. Therefore, it is evident that every year large numbers of distributors have been and are being sponsored into Amway and Shaklee, despite the fact that only a small number of distributors actually recruit new sales agents.

5. Many young people who enter the work force are finding that their jobs simply do not meet their perceived economic needs. Since these young people often lack the

necessary financing (but not the fortitude) to succeed at business, they are prime candidates for multilevel marketing.

6. There is no age barrier for this type of economic venture. A number of middle-aged and older people are seeking the security and benefits of additional income, having found their retirement plans to be inadequate. Multilevel marketing often appeals to them. In fact, I personally am aware of a couple who got involved in Amway when they were sixty-two and built a very lucrative income (in excess of $100,000 per year) in less than three years. They were then essentially able to retire from the business and offer their services on a full-time basis to their church.

7. As more and more people from all walks of life are becoming successful as distributors, the status objections lessen somewhat. Potential recruits are more willing to listen seriously to a presentation regarding the concept. Additionally, the business presentations and training programs have become much more professional and the administrative system has been refined. These factors appeal to someone who is being introduced to the business. It is not surprising that the percentage of distributors remaining from year to year has generally increased, despite the early charges of saturation.

I could continue listing the reasons why multilevel marketing is continuing to experience substantial growth. However, the reasons are less important than is the simple fact that, in the words of the judge in the Amway case and based on the data presented here, the "sales [and compensation] trend has shown almost uninterrupted growth." Thus, despite a fairly high drop-out and inactive rate, the number of active distributors has consistently increased in both Amway and Shaklee since the government's action in

1975. For example, Amway grew from just over 300,000 distributors in 1975 to approximately 1,000,000 in 1981 (a 300 percent increase), while its sales grew even more rapidly. It should be emphasized that it has never been particularly easy for most distributors to sponsor large numbers of people into a legitimate multilevel business, but it can and is being done at a phenomenal rate. A distributor who gets a "no" from a prospect must simply move on. The problem is not "saturation," but rather the fear of failure and all of the related status-oriented doubts. There are always people ready to purchase the products and/or to be sponsored. However, not even the most effective salesperson bats a thousand. If one can accept a negative response as well as a "yes," and is willing to work hard on a consistent daily basis, the potential for sponsoring and selling in a legitimate multilevel marketing business is just as real as it was ten or fifteen years ago.

5

Not All Pyramids Are in Egypt

By the late 1960s and early 1970s, illegal pyramid schemes were being fraudulently developed throughout the United States. In fact, in an article written for the Suffolk University Law Review in the early seventies, it was pointed out that "pyramid sales schemes have been characterized as the number one consumer fraud problem in the United States today [citing testimony of the then-Senator Walter F. Mondale of Minnesota]." The author went on to note that one pyramid scheme alone (Holiday Magic, Inc.) had defrauded a number of investors of "more than $250 million."

The manner in which *some* multilevel marketing arrangements are operated do make them illegal pyramids. Many others, including Amway and Shaklee, are not and never have been illegal. While what constitutes fraudulent pyramiding is a sometimes difficult legal issue, a general review of the history of such schemes and an examination of a few of the relevant cases should assist the reader in understanding what constitutes an illegal pyramid and what does not.

Historically, illegal pyramid activities were (and are) fashioned after the old chain-letter fraud. The chain-letter

45

stratagem is based on the notion that the originator of the scheme writes to a number of individuals, all of whom are to pay him or her a fixed amount of money. After paying the perpetrator (or others higher up on the list), the individuals add their names to the bottom of the pyramid and send the letter on to another group of people. Theoretically, as the letter passes through many hands, those on the top of the list not only recoup their initial "investment" (the amount they paid others for the privilege of becoming part of the chain), but also reap a healthy profit, without rendering any service. Of course, at some point the chain breaks down. Thus, while those at the top of the letter may have made a profit, those at lower levels generally suffer a loss.

In another article, which appeared in the Illinois Law Forum in 1974, a commentator explained how a pyramid scheme operates in certain sales arrangements:

> The pyramid sales scheme, currently a serious consumer fraud problem in the United States, is a new variation on the old chain letter swindle. The investor enters the scheme either by purchasing goods at a greatly inflated price or by paying an entrance fee. In return for his initial purchase or fee, the investor receives the right to a reward for each new investor he finds for the promoter. In the pyramid's simplest form, the reward is a flat fee. In its more sophisticated forms, the reward may be the right to sell products to new investors at a large markup or the right to a fee for each new investor brought into the scheme by those he recruits. No matter how simple or complex the scheme, its essential appeal is the same: the victim is induced to part with his money in the belief that he can make a fortune simply by sending the pyramid promoters a list of names or by persuading a few people to attend a

meeting. Simple arithmetic convinces him that he can become more rich by finding as few as four or five new prospects each month.

In response to the rising number of pyramid "sales" schemes appearing on the scene in the late sixties and early seventies, there were a number of laws passed and legal actions brought to curb such fraudulent practices. Legitimate multilevel businesses such as Amway and Shaklee have suffered unfairly by virtue of the rise of fraudulent get-rich-quick arrangements. Not surprisingly, both Amway and Shaklee have been active in maintaining the integrity of the legitimate multilevel concept by promoting a stringent code of ethics for their distributors and by cooperating in efforts to limit the activities of organizations using fraudulent practices.

Illustrative of the laws devised to curb illegal pyramid ventures is Section 327 of the California Penal Code which makes such ventures a misdemeanor and provides that:

> Every person who . . . operates any endless chain is guilty of a misdemeanor. . . . '[E]ndless chain' means any scheme for the disposal or distribution of property whereby a participant pays a valuable consideration for a chance to receive compensation for introducing . . . additional persons into participation in the scheme or for the chance to receive compensation when a person introduced by the participant introduces a new participant. Compensation . . . does not . . . include payment based upon sales made to persons who are not participants in the scheme and who are not purchasing in order to participate in the scheme.

The same essential rule against fraudulent pyramid schemes was summarized in the case of *In re Koscot*

Interplanetary, Inc., 86 F.T.C. 1180 (1975), *aff'd sub nom,*
Turner v. FTC, 580 F.2d 701 (D.C. Cir. 1978):

> Such [illegal pyramid] schemes are characterized by the
> payment by participants of money to the company in
> return for which they receive (1) the right to sell a product
> and (2) the right to receive in return for recruiting other
> participants into the program rewards which are unrelated
> to the sale of the product to ultimate users.

Based on such rules, the characteristics of an *illegal*
pyramid are clear. The two primary characteristics of
illegal pyramid schemes are: (1) "inventory loading"—the
notion that new recruits must purchase a substantial,
nonreturnable inventory to get involved in the business,
with their sponsor rewarded for the new distributor's
purchase of the inventory; and (2) a "headhunting fee"—
the notion that the new recruit or distributor is to pay a
large sum of money as an entry fee, the sponsor to receive
a portion of that fee. The presence of either or both of these
factors will generally suffice to label an enterprise as an
illegal pyramid. Additionally, there is a third factor that is
almost always present in the case of illegal pyramiding—
the implication that anyone can get rich without working
very hard.

An examination of a few cases should help to illustrate
how these principles work. The case of *State v. Dahlk.* 330
N.W.2d 611 (Wis. Appl. 1983) is an example of a classic
illegal pyramid scheme. In *Dahlk,* an "investor" purchased
a membership in the pyramid club for $1,000 in cash. The
investor then received three manila envelopes, one of
which contained a "tracking sheet" to start a new pyramid
by attempting to sell two memberships. If a membership
was sold, the original investor was permitted to keep $500

and was required to put the other $500 into one of the other two envelopes and pass it to the person whose name appeared on the inside of the envelope (someone higher up in the pyramid or chain). Each of the two new buyers, in turn, were to receive three envelopes and sell memberships to two more people. The process was to continue to the thirty-second position on the pyramid. When each of those thirty-two persons sold memberships to two others, $500 from each of sixty-four buyers would have been given to the investor who had started the new pyramid.

In supporting this pyramiding, the defendant maintained that it depended on the skill and efforts of a given investor to be successful, just as in any other legitimate investment or business venture. The court rejected this claim, holding instead that "the earliest club members, those who enter at or near the top of the pyramid have a greater chance of profiting than do latecomers. Viewing the scheme as a whole, an investor's profit depends on occurrences he cannot control: whether other people induce still others to pay $1,000 to join the scheme; effectively, the club was based on a headhunting fee and on chance." The court, therefore, held that the defendant's pyramid club was an illegal lottery.

An earlier case, *S.E.C. v. Glenn W. Turner Enterprises, Inc.* 474 F.2d 476 (9th Cir. 1973), dealt with another representative illegal pyramid venture, Dare to Be Great, Inc. Under this plan (sales program), promoters offered the public a series of contracts referred to as "Adventures." There were four different Adventures or sales packages. Adventures 1 and 2 contained various basic instructional materials on self-improvement and personal motivation. A purchaser of an Adventure 3 or 4 package, on the other hand, paid a highly inflated fee for additional instructional materials and for the opportunity to receive commissions on the sale of Adventures packages to the public. A purchaser of Adventure 3 could sell Adventures 1, 2, and 3, while a purchaser of the Adventure 4 package could sell Adventures 1, 2, 3, and 4.

Furthermore, to earn his bonus or commission, the Adventure 4 owner did not personally have to obtain a purchaser's signature on a contract. Rather, he or she only had to persuade a prospect to attend a promotional meeting over which the sponsor had no control and did not even have to attend. The promoter would then try to sign up the prospect, and the owner of the Adventure who invited the prospect would receive a commission. The scheme in this case, therefore, required minimal investor effort and also gave the investor only limited control over the operation of the business.

There were elements of both headhunting (a fee was paid for enticing people to come to a meeting, during which they were induced to sign up for an Adventure package) and inventory loading (the new recruit who purchased an Adventure 3 or 4 package paid an inflated amount for materials). The idea that the recruit could make a lot of money without much effort or ability was also present in the Dare to Be Great scheme. It was held to be illegal.

Another case that dealt with a pyramid scheme that developed in the early 1970s was recently decided in California. It was the case of *Bounds v. Figurettes,* 135 Cal. App. 3d 1 (1982). In the Figurettes case, the defendants devised a pyramid system for the sale of women's lingerie, primarily bras, which required fitting. Despite the fact that they could neither fit nor wear bras, a number of men became active in the business by purchasing substantial, nonrefundable inventories. In fact, one publicized recruit was a barber who could not fit or sell the lingerie—and his wife refused to participate in the business. Ultimately, he made monthly purchases of more than $20,000 by sponsoring new recruits and by borrowing to acquire a substantial inventory.

Although there were limited retail sales in this scheme, business was based primarily on the twin evils of inventory loading and payment of a headhunting fee.

In their recruitment materials, the defendants in this case encouraged new recruits to purchase a reserve inventory. A witness further testified "When we didn't have enough money to buy inventory, they [the defendants] said 'Go out and borrow.'" And borrow they did, with some recruits even losing their homes as a result. Additionally, the plan provided that a new recruit could become a direct distributor, receiving a larger bonus, by either building a monthly product volume of $5,000 or by an inventory purchase of $3,000 or more. The court, therefore, had no difficulty in finding that inventory loading existed, even though there was some testimony offered by the defendants about limited sales to consumers.

The court also held that the Figurettes marketing plan involved headhunting. When a new recruit signed up and purchased an inventory, his or her sponsor received a bonus based on that purchase. Thus, the trial court found that the sales were really designed as a recruiting tool to induce the purchase of inventory. Furthermore, the bonuses and discounts encouraged recruiting without regard to actual sales to a consumer.

The court also went to great lengths to add: "By not too cleverly hidden innuendo, prospects were led to believe if they became a counselor they could earn large sums by doing essentially nothing. . . . It is without dispute: representations of easy money were piled on representations of more easy money, coupled with highly emotional, high pressured appeals to greed."

The court held that the defendants' marketing plan constituted an illegal chain scheme, as well as a deceptive trade practice. The appellate court then directed the trial court to enter a judgment of liability and to hold further proceedings to determine the appropriate amount of damages payable to the plaintiff-distributors for the defendants' fraud.

Frankly, in such cases, it is sometimes difficult to sympathize with recruits who are gullible enough to believe that these schemes are a legitimate way of earning money. The obvious efforts to entice new recruits into inventory loading and headhunting, on the promise of easy money, should immediately cause a prospect to question the legitimacy of these scams. However, with high-powered promoting, the irrational nature of these schemes is often hidden in the glittering sales pitch. Therefore, it is appropriate for government to regulate or terminate such illegal activities.

Pyramiding such as that present in the above-mentioned cases is clearly distinguishable from such legitimate multilevel programs as those of Amway and Shaklee. Nevertheless, the legal pressure to control fraudulent pyramiding has had some adverse effect on legitimate organizations.

It is appropriate to illustrate how legitimate marketing programs differ from such scams as discussed above. In fact, there are a couple of court decisions that do precisely that, and I will refer to them.

In the Figurettes case, the defendants tried to assert that their marketing program worked like Amway's compensation plan. The court rejected this assertion outright:

"Amway had avoided the abuses of a pyramid scheme by (1) not having a headhunting fee . . . (2) making product sales a precondition for receiving the performance bonus . . . (3) buying back unsold inventory . . . and (4) requiring a substantial percentage of products be sold to consumers at retail. . . ."

Additionally, in the Amway case referred to at length in chapter 4, although the government had *initially* asserted that Amway was an illegal pyramid, the judge in that case specifically held that Amway was not an illegal pyramid scheme:

> The Amway Sales and Marketing Plan is not a pyramid plan. In less than 20 years, [Amway had] built a substantial manufacturing company and an efficient distribution system, which has brought new products into the market, notably into the highly oligopolistic soap and detergents market. Consumers are benefited by this new source of supply, and have responded by remarkable brand loyalty to Amway products.

The Federal Trade Commission, in an opinion by Commissioner Pitofsky, agreed with the judge's determination. The FTC distinguished the Amway program from a number of illegal pyramids, specifically holding that the Amway Sales and Marketing Plan involved neither headhunting nor inventory loading. It is clear that Amway is not and never has been an illegal pyramid scheme.

Shaklee is not an illegal pyramid, either. The success of anyone in the Shaklee business is directly dependent upon sales to the consumer and involves neither headhunting nor inventory loading. In his book, *The Shaklee Story*, Robert L. Shook notes that—in stark contrast to illegal pyramiding—in a legitimate company such as Shaklee, "no one buys the right to sell. Profit is realized only when products are sold to the consumer; a Shaklee person does not earn one cent by simply sponsoring someone new into the company. Positions aren't bought or sold—nothing influences advancement except performance. . . ."

There are a couple of additional points that should be made to distinguish legitimate multilevel businesses from the illegal pyramid schemes that have tainted the marketplace from time to time. Perhaps most importantly, it takes time and effort to build a successful selling organization in Amway and Shaklee. New distributors must be sponsored and trained, and a solid and consistent customer base must be developed. Rich DeVos and Jay Van Andel, the founders of Amway Corporation, have never said that building a successful Amway business is easy. In fact, they extol the virtues of hard work and the free-enterprise system. Similarly, Lee Shaklee has noted that, in the Shaklee business, "There's no place for the get-rich-quick individual. Shaklee people must care. They must want to give. It's a slow, steady building process—and what they build is solid."

It should also be noted that in both companies new distributors do not work for their sponsors—they work for themselves. Distributors who produce at a rate in excess of their sponsors' can pass the sponsors in terms of income. A sponsor customarily cannot make more money based on the production of a recruit than the recruit does—those who produce reap corresponding rewards. There are literally hundreds of distributors in both Amway and Shaklee who make incomes well into six figures. Many of these successful distributors make much more than their original sponsor—they are not a bottom of a pyramid! Rather, their production and that of their group enables them to rise to a level in the business commensurate with their efforts and capabilities. As often happens, a distributor may make between \$10,000–\$15,000 in gross income per year, while someone he or she has sponsored may earn \$100,000. This is refreshing in a society that increasingly reflects a philosophy which assumes that capable, yet nonproductive, members of society are somehow entitled to share in the productivity of others.

In actuality, the typical large corporation is more of a "pyramid" than are legitimate multilevel businesses such as Amway and Shaklee. There is only one president and one chairperson on the board of directors of a major corporation. In a sense, every corporation has its pecking order, with very few individuals perched at the top. Of course, productivity is normally important in such corporations, but other factors such as internal politics also determine who percolates to the top of the corporate pyramid. Not so with Amway and Shaklee—where production is the only criterion for success.

Finally, those who allege that Amway and Shaklee are pyramids are typically only raising the saturation argument in another form. They argue that lower-level distributors cannot succeed as those at the top can do—because the marketplace is saturated with the product or with distributors. I guess I would have to concede that it is *theoretically* possible for a new distributor to come into a legitimate multilevel business so late in the game that there would be no room for success. However, as a *practical* matter, for both Amway and Shaklee particularly, this would assume that they could gain complete control over household, nutrition, and related worldwide consumer and commercial markets with billions upon billions of dollars of business each year. If this were to occur, it would literally be a boon to millions of distributors. If one really believed there were a threat of this happening, he or she would be foolhardy not to get into a legitimate multilevel business now, to take advantage of that enormous growth. Nevertheless, even if Amway, Shaklee and similar multilevel businesses controlled all their current sales markets, it would be a simple matter to expand into other markets, using the same sales organizations. The growth potential for such marketing programs is almost without limit.

As long as there are products to sell and people to sponsor, reputable multilevel marketing will be a potential source of tremendous amount of income for its participants. Of course, it will be the productive distributors, not necessarily the first to get involved, who will achieve at the highest level. Successful distributors do not expect to "get rich quick," but they do realize that they have the potential of building a very lucrative business arrangement. It is no surprise that those involved seem not to mind that those they sponsor also achieve success which may surpass their own.

6

The Truth Is Good Enough

There seems to be widespread public sentiment that multilevel marketing opportunities are actually or inherently fraudulent. Certainly, there have been and still are multilevel scams, but as was the case with illegal pyramids, all multilevel programs are not intrinsically fraudulent. Rather, there are many highly legitimate marketing opportunities—even though isolated individual sales personnel may occasionally indulge in mispresentation and overstatement without the knowledge of the parent company. This is regrettable—and both Amway and Shaklee, in particular, seek to eliminate such unethical or illegal activities by maintaining fairly strict control of what is proper to include in business presentations through enforcement of their respective codes of ethics.

In this chapter, we will deal with the nature of fraud or misrepresentation, and with the manner in which such improper behavior can be controlled. This information should assist a distributor in detecting even the hint of misrepresentation in his or her presentation of the business.

This chapter will also explain why, as a practical matter,

such misrepresentations (whether intentional or not) only cause a legitimate business to suffer in the long run.

Fraud is defined in *Black's Law Dictionary* as: "An intentional perversion of truth for the purpose of inducing another in reliance upon it to part with some valuable thing belonging to him or to surrender a legal right; a false representation of a matter of fact, whether by words or by conduct, by false or misleading allegations, or by concealment of that which should have been disclosed, which deceives and is intended to deceive another so that he shall act upon it to his legal injury. . . ." As is so often the case, the definition in *Black's Law Dictionary* has endeavored to render a complete legal definition of fraud, but has primarily succeeded only in confusing matters. However, by examining this definition, some clarity can be achieved.

Generally, the legal doctrines of fraud and misrepresentation have evolved for the purpose of prohibiting the use of misleading or deceiving words and conduct in transactions. The basis of this improper deception, in turn, is generally a false representation as to an important fact. In other words, if A induces B to enter into a contract or transaction by misrepresenting a fact that is of material importance to that transaction, A may have engaged in fraud or misrepresentation. Consequently, B may generally sue A to rescind the contract—or for damages, if any have occurred. The essence of fraudulent misrepresentation, therefore, is a *false statement* as to a material fact, coupled with the speaker's *intent to deceive* the recipient or listener.

Some courts, however, have been willing to liberalize this standard, by permitting a recipient to bring an action for fraud, even if the misrepresentation was merely negligent rather than intentional. An even smaller number of courts have been willing to find actionable misrepresentation when the false statement was "innocent," as opposed to being either negligent or intentional. Under any circumstances, to avoid charges of misrepresentation, a party must not only speak the truth but must also engage in some effort to find out what the true facts are before speaking.

As pointed out in the *Black's Law Dictionary* definition, actionable fraud or misrepresentation may occur even when no words are spoken. It may arise when facts that should have been disclosed are intentionally or even negligently concealed. The law will sometimes require a party to disclose facts that he or she knows may be of material importance to the transaction. For example, if the seller of a building covers a termite-infested floor with a rug, thereby concealing evidence of termite infestation from a prospective buyer, the buyer may ultimately be able to rescind his/her purchase of the building or even seek damages against the seller for his/her fraudulent act of concealment. In a somewhat similar sense, if the buyer talks extensively about the virtues of the structural soundness of the building, he/she may also be required by law to disclose any problems in this area. Whether from a failure to disclose or an actual misstatement, the common ingredient in both instances of misrepresentation is the deceptive nature of a presentation.

Fraud or misrepresentation, whether by misstatement or concealment, may come in two forms. "Actual fraud" is active deceit or misrepresentation and is the most common form. "Constructive (or inherent) fraud" is somewhat less common and can be present even though there is neither actual misrepresentation of a fact nor failure to disclose additional facts. Constructive fraud occurs when public policy is violated by an otherwise accurate statement or when the statement carries the very seeds of deception. In other words, therein lies the notion that government should occasionally intervene to protect the public from certain statements that are accurate and yet misleading. For example, the statement that anyone can grow up to be president of General Motors may be technically true, but it could be held to be constructive fraud if someone were to repeat that statement in a manner offensive to public welfare. Constructive or inherent fraud is a very slippery concept, because it relies on an assessment of what is in the public interest.

In addition to both types of fraudulent misrepresentation, an agreement or transaction may be deemed illegal or unenforceable if a party gives his consent under undue influence. Generally, in such cases, it must be shown that a "weaker party was induced [to enter into a transaction or agreement] by unfair persuasion on the part of the stronger [party]." In these instances, it is the bargaining power of the parties and the improper nature of the persuasion involved that may render the agreement unenforceable.

All of these rules have potential applicability in almost any sales context, including multilevel marketing. Sometimes, sales personnel who are overly exuberant, enthusiastic, or downright greedy make misrepresentations of material facts in their efforts to sell the product or program. These material misrepresentations may, in turn, give rise to legal action for rescission or damages, or may result in the termination of the misrepresenting party's distributorship in the case of legitimate multilevel marketing businesses such as Amway and Shaklee. In the case of nonreputable programs their very plan of organization and compensation may be inherently fraudulent. In this chapter we will examine instances of both constructive fraud (inherent deception) and actual fraud or misrepresentation. Either form of activity can be quite detrimental, as both a legal and practical matter, for a distributor and a business. Therefore, I will conclude with an evaluation of the practical, as opposed to strictly legal, implications of misrepresentation or fraud in the multilevel marketing context.

In the Figurettes case, discussed at length in the preceding chapter, the court held that the defendants' marketing plan was inherently deceptive and illegal. In the words of the court: "The plan becomes illegal because it is part of [an] overall marketing plan which depends upon an endless chain of middlemen." Thus, the marketing plan itself was inherently deceptive, regardless of what might be said by a given distributor in a sales pitch.

As mentioned previously, the court in this case distinguished between the illegal Figurettes arrangement and such marketing plans as involved in Amway and Shaklee— on the ground that the latter did not involve sales to an endless chain of middlemen, but rather a very substantial number of sales to consumers. Despite such determinations, there have been some legal efforts to have even legitimate multilevel marketing plans declared fraudulent, as an inherent or constructive matter. In this sense, the government in the previously discussed Amway case initially alleged that, "[Amway's] representations that substantial income or profit may be predicated through . . . unlimited or endless chain increases in the number of distributors or dealers recruited . . . was and is false, misleading and deceptive. . . ." Similarly, in a recent case, the state of Wisconsin alleged that the Amway marketing plan was deceptive because it inherently misrepresents the income potential of the business. Wisconsin asserted that since most new distributors do not reach the Direct level or above (as presented in the business plan), the plan was inherently fraudulent. In effect, Wisconsin argued that when the Amway plan was presented, the representative compensation figures shown, though perfectly accurate, tended to lead a prospect to believe that the figures were *typical* in all cases, not just sample performance levels.

Amway signed a consent decree in the Wisconsin case, thereby terminating the litigation. Amway simply agreed to state the numbers (percentages) of distributors who actually achieve the levels noted in the Amway business presentation. Unfortunately, while much of the national press carried the story of Wisconsin's suit against Amway, they failed to give equal attention to the cooperative resolution of the case.

In a similar sense, the administrative-law judge in the first Amway case held that there was nothing inherently false, misleading, or deceptive about the Amway plan. The Federal Trade Commission essentially agreed, although they did take exception to certain earnings or sales claims. The commission's only problem with the use of specific figures in the Amway plan was that those figures were often allegedly presented as being *typical* rather than merely *attainable.*

Certainly, not every distributor is able or willing to perform at the kind of level described in the presentation of compensation plan. As in any business, it takes hard work to reach the highest income levels. Thus, the average Amway distributor currently has sales of $150 per month, and the average "active" distributor has sales of $454 per month. In fact, in this regard, only 40 percent of Amway's distributors are characterized as "active," and of these, only 35 percent participate in sponsoring and building a business organization. As previously mentioned, many are content to merely purchase the products at a discount and/or sell them to a limited number of customers. (The same phenomenon occurs in Shaklee.) Nonsponsoring Amway distributors tend to bring down the overall level of performance in terms of average sales per distributor. Over 75 percent of the Amway sales force simply do not work very hard at building a sales organization, and their compensation undoubtedly reflects this fact. The remaining distributors, who are involved in both building a sales organization and selling the product, will be more likely to reap the benefits of the Amway plan.

Having illustrated why the hard-working distributor, who is building a sales organization, is likely to reap high economic benefits from the Amway or Shaklee programs, it should be noted that not all such distributors succeed in reaching those levels. But many do, and many more will undoubtedly do so in the future. A person observing presentations of the Amway or Shaklee program should be aware that they are largely intended to explain *how* the compensation and bonus facets of the business work. Even the not-too-perceptive listener should recognize that both sales and sponsoring figures used in presentations are for illustrative purposes. Many distributors achieve more; others, less. The level attained by a particular new distributor is dependent on a number of varied yet predictable factors, not the least of which is how hard he or she wants to work.

In an effort to avoid charges of fraud, Amway, Shaklee, and other legitimate multilevel businesses emphasize that hard work is necessary and discourage their distributors from quoting potential income as "typical." These organizations clearly recognize that their continued survival is based on strict adherence to the truth.

It should be clear from the preceding analysis that legitimate marketing plans do not inherently misrepresent the facts. As previously indicated, these programs, particularly Amway's and Shaklee's, are not inherently deceptive on either saturation or pyramid grounds, since they involve actual sales and sponsoring in expanding markets. Additionally, their presentations are not intrinsically deceptive, because it is clear that the figures quoted do not purport to show how much compensation is actually received by the average distributor.

Although I have very little concern about the basic integrity of legitimate multilevel business plans, I do believe there are occasions when an overly zealous distributor engages in intentional, negligent, or innocent misrepresentation or concealment.

Reputable multilevel businesses such as Amway and Shaklee are very sensitive to this issue. They are aware that there are individuals in their respective sales forces who engage in overstatement and misrepresentation. In an effort to control such practices, Amway and Shaklee and all other legitimate multilevel marketing businesses have promulgated and earnestly seek to enforce a strict code of ethics.

When distributors engage in improper or unethical behavior, they risk termination of their distributorship. Additionally, distributors are subject to legal action if they indulge in actual misrepresentation or fraud. For example, in the Wisconsin Amway case, the corporation was sued, as were four individual distributors. Amway was sued on the ground of constructive or inherent fraud, while the distributors were also subject to suit for actual fraud.

Perhaps the major area in which actual misrepresentation occurs is in the presentation of income figures or by statements that imply that anyone can succeed at the business with very little work. In my opinion, the use of such spurious and exaggerated claims not only subjects the speaker to legal action for intentional or negligent misrepresentation, but also tends to make the business opportunity itself unbelievable. Furthermore, if someone is induced to join the business on such fraudulent grounds, he or she will quickly lose interest in the business upon learning that success does not come so easily. Furthermore, deluded distributors will not only ultimately leave the business, but will leave with bad feelings toward the entire organization. That disillusioned distributor will probably poison the minds of other prospects. When potential distributors are told the truth, they generally sign up properly prepared to work at the business, thus enhancing their potential for success. The very worst that could happen is that the would-be distributor might decide that he or she is not really interested in working that hard. In that instance, the only things lost are a little time and that particular distributor, which would eventually be lost under any circumstances. An enterprising sponsor will usually pick up that prospect as a retail customer, anyway. When there has been no deceit, it is always possible that the prospect will decide later that the business is worth a try, particularly if he or she has been a regular customer in the interim. Furthermore, if a potential distributor has been told the whole truth, whatever the outcome, he or she will probably not bad-mouth the business, but will tend to admire the results of the would-be sponsor's hard work.

Thus, overstating income or other figures is not only legally suspect, it is also counterproductive as a business practice. In the case of a legitimate multilevel business, nothing can substitute for truth. One may reap short-term benefits from deception and innuendo, but ultimate success (as well as a good night's sleep) comes best to those who build on a foundation of truth.

In addition to the potential for actual fraud, there is also a possibility of concealment and nondisclosure. There are times when failing to say something is just another way of leaving the recipient intentionally deceived. Not surprisingly, I oppose concealment just as much as I do false statements, because the effect is precisely the same on legal, moral, and practical levels.

An example of potential concealment or nondisclosure is in order. Concealment would be present, for example, if a distributor made a statement to the effect that his or her last check from the corporation was for $3,000, but failed to point out that bonuses had to be paid from that amount. Without full disclosure, the listener might be led to believe that thé speaker actually made $3,000, when in fact the speaker's share was substantially less. Such a half-truth would clearly be deceptive. Again, I believe such acts of concealment are totally senseless. The listener might be just as impressed with the fact that the recipient made $1,000, or whatever the share might have been, as by the $3,000 figure. Furthermore, a potential recruit would get a better picture of how the business works—the sponsor trains and even pays the "downline" until their businesses have grown to the point where they can be run independently.

In a somewhat similar sense, some detractors of multilevel marketing claim that there is an element of nondisclosure in the manner by which prospects are invited to hear about a business. The prospects are often not told initially what the meeting will be about. In this regard, the Wisconsin suit against Amway also charged that people are often invited to Amway recruitment presentations without a disclosure to them of the true nature of the gatherings. This invitation process is generally referred to as the "curiosity" or "business" approach.

As typically used, this approach involves getting a prospect to attend a sales presentation by such a statement as "we're in the business of helping management-oriented people start their own business," without mentioning the name of the business. In fact, would-be sponsors are sometimes expressly encouraged to completely refrain from mentioning the name of the business.

Although I do not personally believe that the "curiosity approach" is necessary, I can understand why some sponsors persist in using it—and I do not believe that it is necessarily deceptive, as I will explain. As the administrative-law judge in the Amway case noted, the "curiosity approach" developed "primarily in the early 1970s because of adverse publicity about pyramid plans unconnected with Amway." At a time when any multilevel business plan was suspect, certain Amway distributors did not feel that they could get many prospects to a meeting if they knew that it was for the purpose of presenting the Amway Sales and Marketing Plan. Such distributors believed that if they could get a prospect to listen to the whole story, they would have a better chance of gaining a recruit.

There is a widespread though faulty opinion that a multilevel marketing program is a pyramid scam involving a network of door-to-door peddlers. Although this impression is inaccurate, if a would-be sponsor tells a prospect that he or she would like to present the Amway or Shaklee marketing plan, there might be many erroneous first impressions to overcome. Since this is immensely difficult, if not impossible, to do over the telephone or in a brief conversation, the hopeful sponsor might avoid the issue entirely by playing on the prospect's curiosity and not mentioning the name of the business.

In all fairness, both of the faulty first impressions held by some about even legitimate multilevel programs are being overcome by the evidence of successes with companies like Amway and Shaklee. Unfortunately, such impressions do persist in some circles. For example, in an August 18, 1982, article in *Chemical Weekly*, the author referred to Amway as "a company that operates a wide-range network of door-to-door peddlers selling detergent and household products." On the contrary, Amway distributors are strongly discouraged from selling door-to-door. Rather, they sell to friends, neighbors and referrals. Nevertheless, as long as such false impressions exist, it will be difficult to get prospects to listen to the whole story.

The "curiosity approach" may seem to be the only way to overcome the public's misconceptions. When this technique is used, as long as sponsors tell the truth (in other words, they do not *deny* that the business is Amway, Shaklee, or whatever), it might be argued that they are actually furthering the cause of truth. In fact, I personally know a number of successful distributors who assert that they would never have gone to the presentation meeting had they been told what business was to be outlined. Because of their own personal experience, they have become strong advocates of the "curiosity approach," contending that were it not for this method, they would not now be enjoying the rewards they have reaped from their businesses.

Although I personally agree that this approach is not inherently deceptive in a legal sense, I am convinced that it is not necessary. In making this statement, I go against some of the conventional wisdom held by a number of the most successful multilevel distributors. Many highly reputable distributors use this approach, and their integrity and honesty are beyond reproach.

As a practical consideration—without questioning the personal integrity of a sincere recruiter—I simply believe that a more direct approach is preferable. If I were involved in multilevel marketing as a distributor, I would use a telephone approach that would go something like the following:

Me: Hello, Bill. This is Rod Smith. How are you doing?

Bill: Fine, thanks. What's up?

Me: I wanted to invite you and Marge to a business meeting at my house at eight on Thursday evening. Are you free?

Bill: I think so, but what is it all about?

Me: It's an exciting new business concept that I've heard a lot about over the past couple of years, but that I just recently took the time to investigate. It's [Amway, Shaklee, or whatever]. What do you know about it?

Bill: Oh, not much, just the usual. You know, that it's a pyramid or chain-letter deal where you sell products door-to-door. My Aunt Betty was involved a few years ago, but she just couldn't sell the stuff. I'm not interested in selling, Rod.

Me: You know, that's just what I thought, too. But it doesn't work that way at all. I finally took the time to really look into it, and I'm really impressed. I'm sure you'd like to see the whole picture, and I'd like to take about an hour on Thursday to let you have the opportunity. You know I wouldn't be calling someone of your stature, if I didn't really think it was a great business. It may be the best hour away from the television set that you will ever spend.

Bill: Well, I don't know.

Me: Oh, come on. It's only an hour. There's no obliga-
tion on your part, and it really is exciting. You said you
thought you and Marge were available on Thursday night.
How about it?

Bill: Oh, I guess so. But I don't think we'll be interested.

Me: Thanks, Bill. I knew you'd be willing to take a look.
You're that kind of open person. I really appreciate that in
you. See you Thursday at eight.

Certainly, no conversation will proceed exactly like the
prior example, but it does illustrate the essence of my
proposal. I believe that the direct method is the preferable
no-risk approach which can prevent the kind of problems
that might arise when simply appealing to curiosity. For
example, I had a friend who was invited to attend a
meeting at Fred's house. The person extending the invitation was someone other than Fred. Fred was the chief of
police. My friend had no idea what the meeting was about,
because he was not told. As a conscientious citizen, my
friend set aside other plans to attend this meeting at the
chief's home, only to find out that it was a multilevel
business presentation. He was so incensed when he found
out that he had been "tricked" (to paraphrase his words)
that he did not hear much of what went on at the meeting.
I subsequently talked with him and was able to allay some
of his misgivings about the multilevel business in question,
and to assure him that Fred had nothing to do with the
content of the invitation. But he was very soured on the
whole process. I am sure my friend is not alone.

I must concede, however, that the direct method will
not always work on the first try. In fact, it may work less
effectively, at least in the short run, than the "curiosity
approach." It is already becoming fairly difficult to get

people to attend *any* meeting, but the direct approach does have a couple of virtues that may make it very workable over the long haul. For one thing, it is the unabashed truth, and it enables one to speak highly of the multilevel business from the outset. Additionally, it may have some practical benefits. Even if the prospect cancels the first meeting, you can be assured that he or she will be watching your every move in the business. On seeing that it is exciting and that you are having some successes, a prospect will ultimately want to hear more about the venture and will be more likely to be interested when you finally get to sing its praises.

In a sense, I am also arguing for a certain patient persistence. Perhaps I can best explain the direct approach by referring to a biblical passage. In the Gospel of Luke, we read the parable of the widow and the judge who feared neither man nor God.

And he spake a parable unto them to this end, that men ought always to pray and not to faint;
Saying, There was in a city a judge, which feared not God, neither regarded man;
And there was a widow in that city; and she came unto him, saying, Avenge me of mine adversary.
And he would not for a while; but afterward he said within himself, Though I fear not God, nor regard man;
Yet because this widow troubleth me, I will avenge her, lest by her continual coming she weary me.
Luke 18:1–5

Although the Savior related this parable to illustrate the power of prayer, it is nevertheless useful in our case, by analogy. The woman obviously did not entreat the judge in an offensive manner (if she had, he could have easily disposed of her in one way or another). Rather, she was patiently persistent, and the judge knew that he could best deal with the widow by granting her request. Since in our case the request is for only an hour of someone's time, it is likely that he or she will either relent rather quickly to "get it over with" or, preferably, may be willing to put aside any preconceptions and listen with an open mind. Either reaction allows the would-be sponsor the opportunity to present the business in an up-front manner.

Regardless of which approach is used, I believe that one must meticulously avoid even a hint of deception. Most people can simply let their conscience be their guide. A listener can usually sense when a speaker is skirting the truth. In my view, no business is worth that.

Legitimate multilevel businesses do not require stretching the facts. The truth is really good enough. The actual success figures are almost overwhelming, and any embellishment runs the risk of becoming unbelievable. Since the best distributors will soon discover and grow weary of overstatements, misrepresentation may have an adverse effect on their own genuine enthusiasm for the business. If the truth is not good enough to convey the whole picture to a business prospect, nothing will suffice to sponsor and retain that potential recruit.

7

Cover the Down-Side Risk—
And Build Profitability

Just about any business has a risk factor. Major risks in a legitimate multilevel marketing enterprise involve the chance of economic failure (or at least nonprofitability), the uncompensated expenditure of time, and the potential loss in perceived status. These risks can be minimized in the operation of a multilevel distributorship.

Of primary concern to most distributors is the fear that one will invest a lot of money in operating the business, only to see the venture fail to get off the ground and become profitable. However, unlike a franchise or an independent new business, both of which require a substantial capital investment, a new distributorship is very inexpensive—and if the business is operated efficiently, it can and should remain that way. Nevertheless, a multilevel arrangement *can* get out of hand economically and fail to realize profits.

In the case of *illegitimate* ventures, substantial expenses may be required to purchase a distributorship (this is normally referred to as headhunting, whereby a sponsor receives a bonus based on the new distributor's sign-up fee). In addition, substantial up-front expenses may be required to purchase inventory (this is referred to as inventory loading). Although both of these conditions generally make a multilevel business illegal, they are nevertheless present on occasion. My advice in such a case is simple—stay away! Although you might ultimately recoup your losses in a legal action, if you fail economically in operating such a business, the only people that ever seem to benefit substantially from a lawsuit are the lawyers. Most clients (and even some lawyers) suffer both economically and emotionally from prolonged litigation.

Assuming that the multilevel marketing arrangement being considered does not involve inventory loading or headhunting fees, the major threat is the possibility that the business will not be run profitably. A new distributor's sponsor normally provides the best source of information as to how to make money out of the business, but may be a poor source when it comes to showing how that money can be retained as real income.

Many "successful" distributors end up losing money because they do not know how to operate in an efficient, businesslike manner. Although they may achieve a gross profit, they are sometimes not able to maintain a consistent, *net profit* after expenses. This should be of primary concern.

Many distributors with a monthly gross income of $1,000 or more are not presently able to realize a significant net profit.

In fact, in the Wisconsin suit against Amway, it was alleged that many direct distributors in the state ran their businesses at a net loss.

Of course, some people enjoy the trips and other

deductible expenses that can come with the operation of a successful distributorship. Their "losses" are based on the taking of a number of legitimate tax deductions related to operation of their businesses. However, I believe that most distributors want and should make a net profit. The following comments will concentrate on how to maximize net profitability and minimize the risk of economic loss in operating a legitimate multilevel business.

There are two primary ways, in my opinion, of minimizing the down-side factors and maximizing profitability. First of all, one should always endeavor to avoid debt. Second, one should operate the business on a strict budget. There are some exceptions to each of these rules of thumb, but the exceptions are quite rare.

Before commencing my discussion regarding debt and budgeting, I should acknowledge that, in typical lawyer-like fashion, my advice is conservative. In this regard, I would also acknowledge that my suggestions may not be the best way to ensure meteoric growth in a multilevel business—but I am personally convinced that it is a way to maximize the potential for steady and consistent growth with only a minimal risk of failure. An individual distributor should, therefore, carefully weigh my suggestions in the light of his or her circumstances and goals. Distributors and their sponsors should determine what approach seems advisable.

Most new businesses require a substantial financial investment just to get started. Start-up costs vary, but it is almost universally true that any new business (whether by franchising or independently) will require at least a moderate expenditure of funds initially. Furthermore, a typical new business may require further dollar expenditures to remain operational in its early stages—and some ventures never get off the ground in a financial sense.

In some regards, a multilevel business involves similar considerations. It does generally require a small initial investment at the start, although that investment may be refundable. It also requires some ongoing expenses to remain operational, although those can and should be kept to a minimum. However, unlike other businesses, a multilevel distributorship should not run the risk of joining the ranks of the over half a million bankruptcies each year. The expenses are so minimal (and often avoidable), that bankruptcy should never pose a real threat to a distributor. The start-up, operational and maintenance costs of a multilevel business are just too small.

Nevertheless, there are some new distributors who manage to operate their businesses at substantial losses. Typically, they get caught up in the emotional excitement of the business and build up a series of expenses without even realizing it. In fact, oftentimes, their major problem is that they confuse the motivational aspects of their operation with the economics involved. In any marketing context, there is a role to be played by emotion, a definite need for motivation. Such emotion is enormously worthwhile if it is used to help activate a distributor to contact and invite prospects to business meetings or to stimulate sales efforts. However, emotion should not have anything to do with operational expenditures, each of which must be weighed in a businesslike fashion.

In rationally weighing expenditures, with the ultimate goal of keeping them at a level below gross income, it is mandatory that new distributors (or even seasoned distributors who are not able to operate at a net profit) distinguish between necessary and unnecessary expenses. Necessary expenses are those that are actually required to run the business. They may change as one progresses through various stages or levels of a multilevel program.

Thus, both the nature and the amount of expenses for a distributor whose volume exceeds $100,000 are much different from those of a newly recruited distributor. An expense that may be unnecessary in the early stages may become necessary later. Necessary expenses are those presently needed to achieve a specific business purpose. They are planned expenses and based on a proven track record—they are not made in an emotional gush of wishful thinking. For example, a seasoned distributor who regularly sponsors four or five "downline" distributors each month may want to purchase materials in advance for those distributors—while a new distributor without a track record would be foolish to do so. Expenditures should be based on performance not premonition.

Unnecessary expenses, on the other hand, may be roughly defined as those that are not required for operational success at a given point in time. These expenses may be loosely broken down into two categories: (1) expenses for optional items or materials that are not needed now but might be helpful to the business at some future point; and (2) expenses that are simply irrational and imprudent for a particular distributor.

Since the economic resources and personal characteristics of distributors vary, a given expenditure might fall into any one of the three categories (necessary; presently unnecessary but helpful; or imprudent) for three different distributors who otherwise find themselves at the same level in terms of business productivity. In this sense, a distributor who has the money to invest in merely "helpful" materials may be wise to do so, to build the business more rapidly; a person with fewer resources would be ill-advised to follow suit. Even a distributor with the available economic means should approach such expenses cautiously and not fall victim to the faulty notion that materials are equivalent to productivity. This is not true—only effort will make money. Materials such as supplies, inventory, and promotional aids are only tools and are no substitute for personal effort and time investment.

A few concrete examples should help to illustrate my point. Start-up expenses are generally quite minimal. They typically include a sales kit, selected products, and certain very basic operational materials. The sales kit for both Amway and Shaklee is inexpensive—in the range of $20 or less—and normally includes all the information and materials needed to begin building an organization and selling products. In addition to the sales kit, it is generally advisable to purchase an assortment of products that can be used personally and as samples for both potential distributors and retail customers. Finally, in legitimate multilevel marketing businesses, individual sales organizations develop their own techniques and sponsoring materials. It may, therefore, be necessary for new distributors in the group to purchase some of these materials. In this regard, proceed with care. Normally, the amounts paid for the sales kit and for unused products are refundable, but the cost of sponsoring-group material, as opposed to that supplied by the company, may not be. Therefore, if the new distributor uses care in purchasing such sponsoring-group aids (and they are only aids, not essentials) he or she should be able to get started in the business without any substantial, nonrefundable costs. At worst, distributors who are not successful will be left with a modest and partially used assortment of products— purchased below market price—that can still be used or returned.

Before a new distributor purchases a large supply of materials that may represent a nonrefundable investment, there should be a specific use planned for them. For example, if the sponsoring group supplies cassette tapes or other written materials, a distributor should refrain from purchasing a large amount of these sets until sure that he or she will have a sufficient number of interested prospects to warrant the purchase. Furthermore, particularly in a business involving products with considerable consumer appeal, products can be sold at retail to help cover any justifiable expenses. Debt is rarely, if ever, necessary. Some new distributors get involved in multilevel marketing on a shoestring and incur debt to get started—rather than selling a few products to cover their initial expenses. In some instances, they even feel that it is beneath them to sell directly to friends and neighbors. Frankly, if they start with that kind of attitude, they ought to rethink their involvement, for they may be facing a lot of heartache in the business.

If a person has to borrow to get started and is unwilling to recoup the expenses through retail sales, he or she would be wise to find another business.

There are a number of unnecessary expenses that normally should be avoided at the development stage of a distributorship. They include extensive travel, excessive tools, general aids not related to existing specific needs, telephone expenses, newspaper or other advertising, business cards and stationary, and other unrealistic expenditures.

Some new distributors believe that they can best sponsor at a distance. For example, a novice may believe that a cousin who lives 500 miles away might be the best prospect available. The new distributor may immediately phone to arrange a visit to the cousin so that the business can be explained. That is fine—if a trip to see the cousin was already planned and budgeted. (The new distributor could make his presentation at the same time, and then remember to keep future telephone calls to a minimum.) If a trip was not otherwise planned, most multilevel-marketing experts suggest that the trip be postponed. In fairness to both parties, it is far more sensible to sponsor someone closer to home before starting to rack up travel mileage and expenses. Again, new distributors who do not believe that they can sponsor anyone locally should probably stay out of this type of business. As previously discussed, there is no real threat of market saturation, and new distributors are literally being recruited everywhere. Therefore, it makes little sense to travel at great expense, at least in the early stages of the sponsoring efforts. Even when the funds are available, such a trip should not be made until a distributor has had some success in local sponsoring and in generally building a business. This experience will help ensure the cousin's eventual success, as well as that of the sponsor.

On the subject of travel, some sales organizations sponsor seminars and conventions to train and motivate their distributors. Such activities often entail some expenses for travel and lodging. Approach such events with some caution. They are normally very helpful, particularly for those with status difficulties in their business, because they provide the opportunity to see the positive side of the operation firsthand, as one rubs shoulders with, shares conversation, and obtains training from successful distributors. If the trip can be budgeted, it may very well prove worth every dime of its cost—and more. However, when borrowing is necessary for the trip, a distributor should carefully evaluate whether or not he or she is really committed to *working* the business. For distributors not fully committed to doing the often difficult or uncomfortable things necessary for success, such a trip will rarely be helpful and would merely be another unnecessary expense. On the other hand, there are many stories of individuals who lacked the commitment necessary to operate a successful multilevel business until attending such a gathering. Anyone willing to work hard—but wondering if the business really works—would be well advised to attend, if the budget permits.

Nonreturnable selling tools and aids should be purchased with great prudence. Each such purchase should be made only if there is a specific purpose in mind. I would even suggest that the buyer write down the purpose at the time of purchase. Every time a new distributor makes a "helpful though not really necessary" purchase, he or she should be sure that the money is available without borrowing, and that a self-promise is made to actually use those materials. Such expenses should be incurred after rational reflection and not for emotional reasons.

Major or extensive telephone expenses are also not necessary. I would reiterate that it is best to begin building a business close to home. Furthermore, the function of most long-distance telephone calls—to inform or motivate —can generally be met by writing a letter, which is not only less expensive, but normally requires more thought and organization. A letter is a far better means of communicating the desired information. Many distributors spend literally hours on the phone talking with people at a distance. This is usually a counterproductive waste of valuable time and energy. Not only does it result in an exorbitant phone bill, it also takes time away from what you really ought to be doing—sponsoring and working with a local group. Some distributors use the phone to motivate the listener (or themselves). Unfortunately, however, the motivation rarely lasts beyond the telephone call.

The telephone can become a crutch, a device to avoid doing harder and more productive things.

Newspaper and other advertisements are normally unnecessary, but are often used by distributors who are afraid to go out and meet a prospect face to face. If a distributor is unwilling to issue an invitation in person, it is extremely unlikely that he or she will be successful at the business. Advertisements will not do for distributors what they need to do for themselves, which is to get out to meet and recruit distributors. I have heard some distributors say that they use ads because they do not know enough people or because they are shy. Again, their problem will not be solved by an ad, since it serves only to insulate them from the real problem. The best way to overcome shyness is to set a goal of meeting and contacting others and then go out and try to achieve it. In this sense, a multilevel business can be a great way of facing one's real fears, because as each one is overcome, personal growth occurs.

Business cards, stationery, and personalized printed devices generally constitute another needless expense at the developmental stage of a multilevel business. Ultimately, since such supplies are fairly inexpensive, not too much harm will be done by purchasing them. However, they generally represent a deeper issue. Just as newspaper ads may be a futile effort to deal with one's shyness, business cards and the like may be used to overcome a status problem. Some distributors believe that imprinted cards are needed to give a business credibility—or at least to add stature to their own involvement. In my opinion, participation in a reputable business such as Amway or Shaklee does not require printed stationery or cards in the early stages of building the operation. No business card ever sponsored a new distributor or sold a product! Furthermore, using a card to soften a distributor's own insecurity may be counterproductive, since it is better to face the initial doubts directly and later reward oneself for success.

The final category of unrealistic or imprudent expenditures includes all those that do not directly relate to a specific business purpose—anything from a new wardrobe to a new Cadillac. If you really want such items and can afford them, buy them—but do so with the understanding that they will not build your business for you.

A distributor may ultimately want to purchase some unnecessary but desirable items at a later stage in the business, to fulfill a dream or as a reward for prior productivity. For example, I have a good friend who is involved in multilevel marketing with his wife. He recently purchased a Cadillac for her. He was in a financial position to do so, since over a period of a few years, he and his wife had built their multilevel business to a point where it was profitable enough to absorb the cost of the new automobile easily. At that point in time, his wants and his means were compatible. He wanted to reward his wife and, in the process, reward himself. They both had earned an economic reward, by virtue of their past performance and their present commitment. They had made one of their dreams a reality through hard work—and did not try to live that dream before it was realistic to do so. Since the dream of a new car had motivated them to do the things necessary to build their business, it was not a foolish expenditure.

A few final remarks regarding debt are now in order. During the inflation of the seventies, there were those who recommended business-incurred debt as a viable means toward economic security. Although this may have worked in a limited number of instances during that time, it has never been true of multilevel marketing, which contemplates compensation for actual production, not theoretical paper earnings of the type fueled by inflation. Furthermore, even those who then advocated building fortunes on paper (financial statements) have had to modify their position in the eighties.

At any rate, in the multilevel context, debt should be avoided in virtually every instance. If one watches both debt and expenses in beginning a multilevel business, a profit may be turned very early. In this light, I believe that there is a great psychological (as well as economic) benefit to realizing a net profit as soon as possible. When money is made from the start, it is easier to keep business growth in perspective. Since building a strong multilevel organization requires continual effort, a consistent system of rewards can be very helpful, even if small at the outset. For example, a person making a net profit of $50 the first month, $100 the second month, and $175 the third month can see the growth potential of the business firsthand. I have intentionally used fairly small figures to illustrate a further point. An additional net profit of only $175 in one month can be a great stimulus to a new distributor, particularly when that income is earned on a part-time basis and is added to an already existent and fairly static income. Netting the extra $175 can make a large difference in one's purchasing power, possibly allowing for a down payment on a house or a better car. That early profit can stimulate a new distributor to further effort as he or she recognizes the real profit potential of the business. Committed distributors will build on prior foundations, in terms of both retail sales and organization.

Of course, if a distributor can afford to put all or a substantial portion of the profits back into the business to purchase necessary or merely helpful materials, it should help build the business more rapidly—provided the new materials are used as part of the overall plan. However, even in such cases, I would often recommend that a small portion of the profits be used to purchase something as a tangible reward for past efforts.

My discussion of limiting debt is also directed to established and successful distributors. Debt has two sides for them. On the one hand, they, too, must avoid personal debt and watch their expenses in the interests of maximizing the profit potential of their business. On the other hand, they need to help their "downline" watch their own debt handling—not only because distributors whom they have sponsored will be more satisfied with the business when it turns a net profit, but also because a sponsor is often the creditor for such debt. Debts owed to a sponsor can easily get out of hand and can result in unhappiness for all concerned. "Cash and carry" is the best policy.

The preceding discussion leads naturally into my next recommendation. One way to avoid debt is to organize finances through strict adherence to a planned budget. With the help of a sponsor or someone else who is successful in the multilevel business, a distributor should sit down and organize a budget, listing all of the expected expenditures. With the advice of someone experienced in the business, it should be possible for even a new distributor to budget fairly effectively from the very beginning— and it will be easier later on.

In budgeting, it is necessary to list all anticipated expenses, allocating a projected amount for each expense on a weekly or monthly basis. This amount will change, as the demands of the business shift, or as the distributor gains more experience. The very act of writing down the anticipated expenditures will help the distributor to think in a businesslike fashion about his or her financial expectations.

As each expense is considered (rationally, not emotionally), it will be helpful to think about the purpose of that expenditure, to consider what needs to be done to turn that expense toward a productive purpose. If one anticipates an expense for materials to be shown to prospects, there should be a list of those prospects and an actual program in mind (and preferably on paper), by which that purpose can be met during the applicable budget period. If the expenditure is not *necessary* to the achievement of a specific purpose, it should not be funded.

In a related sense, I recommend that every distributor keep a daily log, or at least a weekly journal or diary, in which he or she lists the day's specific business goals and describes the efforts to reach those goals. To best achieve this result, the goals for each day should be written in the journal at the beginning of the day (or at the close of the previous day). In turn, the daily entry of efforts expended should be written at the close of the day (or at the beginning of the next). In this way, goals and efforts can be evaluated and new goals set accordingly.

An example may be helpful. I have selected a one-day period, July 15. The goals for that day are entered that morning, or on the night of July 14—at the same time as are listed the activities of July 14. Later, the efforts made on July 15 will be summarized and evaluated in light of that day's goals. This can be done that same night or on the morning of July 16. Here is a sample entry:

BUSINESS GOALS
(written on the morning of July 15 or previous night)

1. Call Bill and Marge. Invite them to Thursday's meeting.
2. Add three new prospects to my contact list.
3. Study the compensation plan and practice presenting it.

ENTRY

(written on evening of July 15 or the next morning)

1. I finally got up the nerve to call Bill and Marge. Bill said he wouldn't be available on Thursday, and I said I would call him back to set a better time.
2. I added three prospects to the list—my dentist, Frank and Jane Myers, and Pat Dominguez.
3. I also studied the plan, but did not have time to practice it.

I believe that it is rare that more than three or four goals can be achieved on any given day. Most leaders in multi-level marketing acknowledge that a long list often becomes depressing and self-defeating. It is best to make a short list of goals that are attainable in the designated period. Consistency, again, is far better than periodic flashes in the pan.

In my hypothetical example, I failed to achieve my goal of having Bill and Marge come to the Thursday meeting and also was unable to practice the presentation. Since both of these matters are important, they should be continued on the list of the goals for July 16. Other goals should be added for that day, as well. Achieving just two or three goals on a daily basis can bring phenomenal results in the long run. Success comes in small steps—here a little, there a little—not in great gushes.

I also believe that one should include in the journal misgivings such as "I finally got up the nerve." It is important to think about your feelings and to take pride in overcoming your fears or apprehensions. Furthermore, if one becomes successful, such honest journal entries may help in training and counseling new distributors. It is always nice to be able to say, "I know just how you feel. I felt the same way when I first called Bill and Marge. But I sure felt good after I did it. I had accomplished something that was very hard for me to do, and regardless of how Bill and Marge reacted, I felt good about overcoming my hesitations."

I recognize that debt, budgeting, and keeping a journal comprise some of the less glamorous aspects of the business. However, successful distributors often note that precise attention to these details may give a new distributor a competitive edge. Involvement in multilevel marketing is a business and should be treated as such, including attention to the utilitarian items that characterize the day-to-day operation of any successful venture. There are a number of entertaining facets to a multilevel business, but there are also some matters that require strict attention and hard work. I have spent a considerable portion of this chapter dealing with the economic aspects of operating a multilevel business. It should already be obvious that an equally important determinant of success in this type of business is the wise investment of time.

Writing a daily journal, reflecting on budget items, and visualizing goals represent time well spent on a business. One of the major problems with most new distributors, however, is that they simply do not budget their time and, consequently, spend too many hours running around in circles for no observable purpose. Using time effectively will increase both one's profit potential and pleasure in the business.

If a new distributor seriously reflects on his or her use of time and discusses time scheduling with a successful "upline" distributor (one on a higher level, not necessarily the original sponsor), it is possible to minimize the likelihood that the new distributor will waste much less time in the future. Normally, new distributors who approach their "upline" in a businesslike fashion and request assistance in time utilization will find the veteran distributors very willing to counsel them.

Although some distributors may appear to reach success without organizing their time very effectively, the vast majority of top distributors are excellent time managers. They have learned that success comes most easily when activities are carefully planned and scheduled realistically in the hours allotted for the business. Time, like dollars, should be carefully allocated with a specific business purpose in mind.

We have seen that wise management of debt, sound budgeting, and specific planning can minimize the possibility of failure in a multilevel business. When those danger areas are under control, only one potential risk remains—the possible loss of status.

As explained in chapter 3, many people are reluctant to get meaningfully involved in even a legitimate marketing program because they believe that outsiders may look down on them. The Greek philosopher Heraclitus noted this phenomenon, albeit in a different context, when he noted that "dogs bark at strangers." In a sense, anyone who gets involved in a multilevel business has become a stranger and will have to listen to the "dogs bark" at him. Fortunately, however, not all dogs bark—some are converted. I suspect that very few people would let a barking dog stand in the way if they saw a pot of gold within their reach. This is precisely the attitude a new distributor must take. The barking dogs may turn some people away, but not those who are willing to risk listening to the barking to reach a desired goal. The dogs bark but they seldom bite. Perceived loss in status, like the bark of a dog at a stranger, is rarely followed by a physical bite. Friendships are rarely lost, and any perceived reduction in status is hardly harmful, although it may be humbling.

Paul Conn, author of several books dealing with the Amway experience, notes, "The dogs bark, but the caravan rolls on." Legitimate multilevel businesses are the caravan, and they will continue to roll on, producing one success story after another. For those who succeed, the status objection begins to evaporate in proportion to the economic rewards. At any rate, the dogs bark because they see something strange, not because the direction taken by the caravan is wrong. Dogs barked and people chuckled when a few G.I.'s purchased stock in Honda, a Japanese motorcycle company, at the close of World War II. The noise kept some away, but others were willing to try. Those who tried, won. Those who did not, lost nothing but a great opportunity. In this light, my suggestion is to ignore the barking and keep an eye clearly fixed on the desired goal. Many distributors in legitimate multilevel marketing businesses come to appreciate that the possible loss of perceived status is the least costly of all risks.

With very few exceptions, I am personally impressed with the quality of the people I have observed in legitimate multilevel businesses such as Amway and Shaklee. These ventures are wonderful opportunities with very minimal economic risks, and the participants tend to be very supportive of one another. This is a pleasant combination in today's world.

Thus, if a distributor keeps debt to a minimum, budgets both time and money in a realistic manner, while selectively ignoring any perceived loss in status, he or she may enjoy a fairly risk-free business and earn a substantial income in the process. The down-side risk is minimal and the up-side potential is tremendous.

8

A Business—
Not a Tax Shelter or a Hobby

The central theme of this book is that legitimate multi-level organizations offer an attractive and potentially profitable opportunity for individuals who are interested in going into business for themselves. Like other business ventures, the operation of a multilevel marketing business may have tax implications.

Before turning to the tax implications, a couple of points should be emphasized. Multilevel marketing is a business opportunity; it is not a tax shelter, although some distributors have improperly tried to sell it as such. In fact, Representative Stark, an influential member of the House Ways and Means Committee, initiated investigation of reports to the effect that people involved in some direct-selling programs were promoting their operations as tax shelters, rather than as profitable business opportunities. Representative Stark stated that his decision to investigate was precipitated by a telephone call that he received early one morning. The caller asked him, "How would you like to make a hundred thousand dollars tax-free?" Stark relates that his first thoughts were that someone was trying to entice him into some shady Abscam-type deal.

91

Actually, it turned out that he was merely being contacted by an overzealous distributor involved in multilevel marketing. This approach caused the congressman some concern because it smacked of potential tax evasion. Based on these suspicions he initiated hearings regarding the tax status of multilevel and other direct-selling businesses. Commissioner Egger of the Internal Revenue Service is also reported as having said that he believed that many direct-selling participants use the tax-benefits or tax-shelter approach to induce individuals to get involved in multilevel marketing. Based on this belief, the IRS has targeted a number of people involved in multilevel marketing for a special tax audit.

Legitimate multilevel organizations such as Amway and Shaklee have repeatedly sought to eliminate the "tax shelter" myth. In fact, in a recent legal bulletin, Amway Corporation responded to a question as to whether it is proper to say that an Amway distributorship is a form of "tax shelter," as follows:

> Absolutely not! Recently several self-styled tax experts speaking on privately produced tapes or so-called tax seminars have stated that, as an Amway distributor, you can convert certain personal expenditures into permissible, deductible business expenses. It is this concept of converting "personal expenses" into "business expenses" that has been referred to as a "tax shelter." Promoting Amway as a "tax shelter" is a distortion of the Amway Sales and Marketing Plan and cannot be tolerated. Amway is a business-building, profit-generating enterprise and should be promoted only in that way.

Legitimate multilevel businesses recognize that such exaggerations of the tax implications or underlying purposes of multilevel marketing are improper, both legally and morally.

Such overzealousness on the part of some distributors poses a threat to the tax status of all distributorships. Representative Stark, for example, has indicated that he is considering advocating a change from the present tax approach—which requires disclosure and documentation of all business-related deductions or tax savings on the part of a distributor—to an approach that would limit the maximum allowable amount of deductions to the amount of annual receipts derived from a distributor's business activity. Such a proposal, advocated in response to the excesses of a few, would be very harmful to many distributors, particularly to newer distributors, who may incur expenses in excess of income in the process of getting his/her business underway.

To avoid such restrictions and to maintain the integrity of their operations, legitimate multilevel businesses seek to place constraints on the excesses of their distributors. Just as lawyers and doctors are learning that if they do not police themselves, the government will, people involved in legitimate marketing businesses are learning that if they do not curb their own immoderate behavior, stringent and often unfair government intervention is inevitable.

Aside from the practical, political, and legal problems that have arisen as a result of trying to sell multilevel marketing as a tax shelter, another somewhat related difficulty emerges. Selling a multilevel marketing opportunity as a tax shelter, rather than as a potentially profitable business venture, may often induce distributors to incur needless expenses in the belief that they are building tax savings rather than a business. Each expenditure should be evaluated from a profitability standpoint, not solely as a tax loophole. At best, tax considerations are a secondary by-product of efforts toward business growth. At worst, excessive emphasis on tax considerations sometimes serves to divert a distributor's attention from his or her real purpose—to build a profitable and secure business.

There is yet another problem related to the operation of a multilevel business that may have tax implications. Frankly, I have observed some distributors who conduct their operations more like a hobby than a business. They characteristically do not expend much effort, working only on an irregular or inconsistent basis—when they feel like it. With this inconsistency in effort, many of these distributors find that their hobby, like most hobbies, produces expenses that exceed income. Some aspects of running a multilevel business ought to be fun, but if that is its primary purpose, it is unlikely to become profitable. It is also likely that the expenses in excess of profits incurred in the venture will not be legally deductible for tax purposes.

If a distributor does not carry on the direct-selling activity for the purpose of making a profit, it will not be considered a business for tax purposes by the IRS. Therefore, the tax deductions and benefits enumerated in the remainder of this chapter may be limited by the IRS to the amount of income earned from the business. This is what has been termed the Not-for-Profit Limit by the IRS. Expenses incurred in furtherance of a nonbusiness or hobbylike venture are not deductible to the extent that they exceed income generated from the business. Thus, the hobby attitude with which some distributors approach their operations may inhibit the growth of their business, as a practical matter, and may also eliminate anticipated tax savings, as a legal matter.

The IRS considers a number of factors in determining whether or not one's effort is deserving of treatment as a business or as a hobby. None of the factors, standing alone, is normally decisive, but are instructive when taken collectively. Among the factors considered are the following: (1) whether the distributor carries on his direct selling in a "businesslike" manner; (2) whether the time and effort expended on a multilevel business indicates an intent to make it profitable; (3) whether losses are due to circumstances beyond the distributor's control or are normal in the start-up phase of direct-selling; (4) whether the distributor changes methods of operation in an attempt to improve profitability; and (5) whether the direct selling related to one's business results in a profit in some years.

It should be clear, therefore, that there are practical business and tax reasons for seeking to make one's business profitable. That should be the major reason for involvement in multilevel marketing. Since other sections in this book deal with actual operational techniques that can enhance profitability, I will now turn to the tax aspects of operating such a business. However, before doing so, I want to put these tax aspects in perspective—they are but a secondary part of building one's profitability.

In the remainder of this chapter, I will discuss the various general tax aspects related to owning and operating a successful multilevel business. In the following chapter, I will indicate some techniques of record keeping that are essential not only to document deductible expenses but as a recommended business practice. Legitimate and legally acceptable tax deductions and credits must be distinguished from "tax evasion." As previously noted, overstating the tax aspects may lead to significant problems. I will, therefore, endeavor to enumerate the tax deductions in a direct and yet conservative manner. Since the material covered in this chapter could easily be expanded to fill an entire book, my advice will necessarily be general. Therefore, I strongly suggest that anyone operating a multilevel business obtain specific and competent advice from a tax lawyer or accountant to ensure that he or she receives the full and legally allowable tax deductions.

I also recognize that many distributors believe that they cannot afford specialized tax advice. While this may be the case in some instances, it may not be true when significant business expenses are anticipated. For those distributors who are just beginning, but who do not anticipate incurring extensive business expenses at the early stages of developing their businesses, I would strongly recommend that they obtain and carefully review Publication 911:Tax Information for Direct Sellers, developed by the IRS with input from the Direct Selling Association for use in 1983. This bulletin and other tax information is obtainable from the IRS, and similar material is also available from reputable multilevel-marketing organizations. I believe, for example, that both Amway and Shaklee corporations have materials to assist distributors in familiarizing themselves with the basics of the pertinent tax rulings. However, I would advise against using tapes or other materials that are circulated by a sales organization or used in a seminar if not sponsored by the parent corporation. Since some of these materials may contain overstatements and inaccuracies, they are to be avoided.

A multilevel business enables active and sponsoring distributors to deduct many expenses incurred in developing the profitability of their business. These deductions can be loosely categorized as follows:

1. Travel and transportation expenses for business purposes.
2. Entertainment expenses, including gifts, meals and other such expenditures if they are actually business related.
3. Certain housing costs—subject to strict limitations—when a portion of one's home is used *exclusively* for an office or for storage purposes.
4. Wage and salary deductions for employees.
5. Retirement plans, including pension and Keogh plans.
6. Business-related equipment such as typewriters, copiers, video equipment, and computers used primarily for business purposes.

Each of these categories will be discussed.

1. Travel and Transportation.

When these expenses are incurred primarily for business purposes, they are deductible. For example, when a distributor operates an automobile in connection with his or her business, the operational expenses may be deductible, provided they are appropriately documented. The deduction for the operation and maintenance of a vehicle used in such a business can be taken in either of two ways.

On the one hand, a taxpayer may compute actual automobile or related transportation expenses to determine the business amount deductible. These expenses may include depreciation as well as the actual costs of operating a vehicle. Deductible operating and maintenance expenses include (but are not necessarily limited to) the cost of gas, oil, repairs, and related expenses. If the vehicle is used only partly for business, the expenses must be apportioned between those for deductible business purposes and those for nondeductible personal use. In order to make such an allocation, one must keep a strict record of mileage used for each purpose. To determine the percentage of business miles driven, one divides the number of business miles by the total miles driven that year and multiplies the result by 100. This percentage is applied to the total operational expenses to arrive at the amount deductible for business purposes. For example, if the total documented expenses related to operation of a given vehicle are $4,000, and the percentage of business use based on yearly mileage figures is 70 percent, the amount deductible would be $2,800 (.70 x 4,000). Validating such a deduction requires strict maintenance of mileage records for business purposes and detailed documentation of operational expenses.

In addition to operational expenses such as gas and oil, repairs, tune-ups, tires, insurance, and registration fees, there may be available a deduction for depreciation of a vehicle used for business. The IRS requires depreciation of assets with a useful life of more than one year. Cars generally fall into the three-year-useful-life category and may often be depreciated over that period of time. Depreciation may, in turn, be taken on an accelerated or straight-line basis. For example, let us assume that a distributor bought a new car for $10,000 on September 15 and drove the car 3,000 miles before the end of the year, including 1,200 miles for business purposes. The allotment for business use would be 40 percent (1,200 ÷ 3,000). If the owner decides not to use the standard mileage rate, the car will be treated as three-year property under the ACRS (Accelerated Cost Recovery System), which provides for a depreciation deduction of 25 percent of the car's basis during that year. Because the distributor drove the car only 40 percent for business, only 40 percent of this amount or $1,000 ($10,000 × .25 × .40) can be deducted as depreciation.

Alternatively, rather than keeping the records necessary

to prove the actual amount of the deductible expense, as outlined above, a distributor may, based on 1984 figures, take a preestablished IRS annual deduction of 20.5¢ per mile for the first 15,000 business miles and 11¢ per mile for the mileage over 15,000. For example, if the total business-related mileage was 10,000 miles, a total deduction of $2,050 could be taken.

Either one of these methods can add substantially to one's legitimate tax deductions. However, since the two computations of deductible vehicular expenses will usually produce different figures, and since the figures will vary according to mileage accumulated, the value of the car used, and other related factors, I would suggest that a distributor keep meticulous records of both mileage and expenses, so that at the end of the year he or she can select the method that will produce the greatest net tax benefit. (Under certain circumstances, a tax investment credit may also be applicable.)

Since the tax laws related to business expenses change quite often, it is advisable to seek specific advice from a competent tax advisor regarding what expenses are allowable in an individual case.

In addition to automobile and related transportation expenses, some business-related travel expenses are also deductible. Food, lodging, and even incidental expenses such as laundry are deductible for business travel in the United States. To qualify for such deductions, the travel must be for a business purpose—and the taxpayer must have been away from home overnight. As was the case with basic transportation expenses, a multilevel business may generate substantial travel deductions. However, again, these expenses must be adequately documented and are deductible only when the primary purpose of the travel was to benefit one's business.

For example, if a distributor lived in Fresno, California, and was invited by a sponsor to attend a weekend rally in San Diego, he or she could deduct reasonable out-of-pocket expenses for the trip. If the distributor received a program or other material outlining the substance of the event, these materials, notes taken at the meeting, and all receipts should be retained to establish the business purpose of the travel. In 1983, the IRS began to permit taxpayers to deduct a specified amount per day for meals while traveling away from home for business, without requiring that the actual cost of each meal be substantiated. However, since the entire cost of business travel to and from destinations within the United States is normally deductible, it is critical to document the business purpose for such travel.

Foreign travel is treated differently than travel within the United States, as a more stringent set of rules must be satisfied to qualify for deductibility. For travel abroad, the taxpayer must normally apportion all costs, including travel expenses to and from the foreign destination, between personal and business purposes. However, such strict allocation, requiring rather precise documentation, is not generally required if less than 25 percent of the taxpayer's time is spent on personal activities. Additionally, when a taxpayer is an employee who lacks control over the destination of the foreign travel and is reimbursed for expenses by the employer, nonreimbursed expenses may be deductible. Of course, new distributors will rarely engage in international travel to build their businesses. Since the costs are prohibitive, such travel should generally be discouraged until a distributor has a thriving business. Therefore, distributors who are contemplating a foreign trip for the purpose of building their business

should seek specific tax advice from a qualified accountant or tax lawyer before taking the trip.

2. Entertainment.

In addition to transportation and travel expenses, a
person involved in a multilevel business may often deduct
entertainment expenses as well. Again, documentation of
the business nature of such expenses is required. One
commentator has referred to the rules for deducting
entertainment expenses as "a maze of dotting the i's and
crossing the t's." Essentially, however, the five W's must be
documented: (1) Whom he/she met with; (2) Where they
met; (3) When (the date) they met; (4) What expenses were
incurred; and (5) Why (business purpose) the expense was
incurred.

Reasonable entertainment expenses directly related to
"maintaining or promoting" one's business are normally
deductible. To prove that such deductions are legitimate,
the taxpayer must be able to show that the expenses were
directly related to or associated with the active conduct of
the business. The terms *directly related* and *associated
with* are defined in detail in tax materials and must be
strictly complied with in order to obtain the deduction. If
the main purpose of the entertainment or meal was
personal, it is not deductible, even if some business was
conducted. As a moral and a legal matter, I would stress
the importance of evaluating and documenting such expenditures to establish whether they were personal or
business in nature.

Certain business gifts may also be deducted. Deductible
business gifts made during the tax year to any one
individual may not exceed $25 in value. While the deducti-

ble amount given to any one person during the year is limited to $25, the total number of gifts that may be given to a number of individuals is not. As with all business deductions, however, the business purpose of the gift must be documented.

3. Housing Costs.

The next major category of tax saving involves certain deductions for maintaining a business office in one's home. Due to abuse of this provision, the tax rules permitting these deductions have been tightened to eliminate excesses. Nevertheless, with proper record keeping and strict adherence to the applicable regulations, the taxpayer may allocate certain home expenses for business uses. Essentially, in order to qualify for the business-in-the-home deduction, the taxpayer must meet the following requirements: (1) a portion of the home must be set aside for *regular* and *exclusive* use in the business; (2) the home area used must be the principal business location; and (3) the amount of the deduction may not exceed the gross income from the business use of the home. It should be noted that the IRS has modified the third requirement in a recent letter ruling. In that letter, the IRS has asserted that it will disallow the office-in-the-home deduction if the taxpayer reflects a loss on Schedule C of his/her income tax return. Although these three requirements are strictly enforced, many distributors are able to set up and document the office-in-the-home deduction. When this can be done, a significant tax deduction may be available.

The way a qualified deduction works is relatively simple. To calculate the percentage of the home used exclusively and regularly for business purposes, one must compare the area used for business with the total area of the home.

Many distributors are able to take a deduction for a garage, basement, or similar area used for storing products and also office space used exclusively for business purposes. For example, if the total area of the home is 2,000 square feet, and the taxpayer is using a garage of 100 square feet for product storage or distribution, plus a room which is 100 square feet as an office area, he or she can receive a deduction for that space. Since 200 square feet is 10 percent of the total area, if household expenses (utility costs and home insurance premiums, for example) totaled $6,000 for the year, the taxpayer could deduct $600 of that expense. It should be reemphasized, however, that there would have to be sufficient income from the business to offset the $600 deduction.

4. Wage and Salary Deductions.

Payments made to employees for services rendered may be deducted for tax purposes, although these payments are often subject to various reporting requirements. "Wages" paid to one's children who are actually employed in the business may be deducted, provided that the compensation is reasonable and the services performed are necessary. There is a whole body of case law related to what is a necessary or reasonable expense, however, and I would suggest that distributors seek competent tax advice before putting their children to work as employees in their business.

5. Retirement Plans.

It is also possible to realize major tax savings by deferring a portion of one's income through the maintenance of a Keogh or pension plan. The potential earnings from Amway, Shaklee, or other reputable marketing organizations provide a distributor with the opportunity to retire on income from the business after developing a significant, ongoing operation. Effective distributors train a "downline." Distributors on lower levels, in turn, learn to train their own "downline." After a period of time, a particular distributor's group may become self-sustaining. Eventually, there are so many well-trained and successful distributors that the group's business will be productive despite the fact that the distributor who started the ball rolling begins to do other things. At that time, the original distributor can effectively retire or at least reduce his or her involvement in the business. In practice, very few successful distributors choose to do this, since they come to enjoy both the material rewards and the feelings of satisfaction that accompany active participation in a thriving multilevel business.

Having briefly discussed the actual retirement potential of multilevel businesses, I will turn to the somewhat related topic of creating a tax-beneficial retirement plan. When I was in private practice a few years ago, many of my clients considered incorporating their businesses for tax-related purposes. One of the major tax benefits available upon incorporation was the possibility of creating a corporate pension plan for officers and employees of the corporation. This pension plan, in turn, would normally permit the taxpayer to defer taxes on the portion of income that qualified for pension purposes. In addition, the income generated within the plan would normally not be taxable until withdrawn. Such benefits were often a major inducement for a businessperson to incorporate.

Today, however, Congress has sought to extend relatively similar benefits to noncorporate business operations, through broadening the contribution base for Keogh plans. The tax value of such pension contributions can often be quite substantial. Three significant facets of a Keogh arrangement make it very attractive: (1) the annual amount invested is normally not treated as taxable income for that year; (2) the income earned on the accumulated amount in the plan over the years is normally not taxable in the year it is earned (therefore, the value of the total in the pension often grows rapidly); and (3) the taxpayer can usually retain some control over how the funds placed in the plan are invested. However, the funds may not be withdrawn until a specified age without being treated as income and subjected to substantial tax liability.

Many tax lawyers and accountants used to advise incorporation fairly regularly for successful small businesses, so that their owners could take advantage of tax benefits related to corporate plans. However, as of 1984, it may no longer be necessary in most instances to incorporate to take maximum advantage of pension planning. The rules regarding Keogh plans (which are pension plans with similar tax benefits, but which do not require incorporation) have been liberalized, effectively eliminating for many taxpayers the distinctions between Keogh and corporate pension arrangements. Beginning January 1, 1984, the yearly contribution limit on Keogh plans was raised from $15,000 to $30,000, although the amount may not exceed 15 percent of one's net annual income. Such deductions may lower one's tax bracket as well as reduce overall tax liability. These benefits are available to any self-employed person or operator of a small business, and the tax savings may be of significant value to individuals involved in multilevel marketing.

6. Business Equipment.

The purchase of certain business equipment, such as a typewriter, copier, computer, or possibly even a video recorder, may also qualify as tax deductions. It is highly advisable to consult a tax expert to determine whether or not a specific purchase in this category is covered under current tax rulings. Under certain circumstances, the total purchase price may be deducted in the year of purchase. In other cases, the equipment must be depreciated on a five-year schedule stipulated by the IRS.

In the preceding discussion of the potential tax benefits accruing to a person involved in multilevel marketing, I touched on several basic deductions or tax write-offs. Each of these areas may represent actual tax savings to a distributor, but there are complex rules regarding documentation and other aspects of substantiating the deductions or credits claimed. I should therefore reiterate the importance of obtaining competent tax advice in each of these areas and regarding other deductions that may be allowable. Competent tax advice entails much more than a rushed, end-of-year preparation of a tax return. It requires advice and assistance in setting up, documenting, and maintaining tax records throughout the year. Furthermore, since tax law is ever-changing, information contained in this chapter may soon become outdated. Good tax advice on a regular basis is therefore essential to the operation of a successful multilevel business.

9

The Basics of Record Keeping

It should be obvious that documentation is an essential requirement for maximizing and verifying the tax savings outlined in the previous chapter. However, effective record keeping is important for general business growth as well, since it helps a distributor plan his or her time and effort in a businesslike and prudent manner. Since most distributors begin their multilevel business activity on a part-time basis, it is essential that they use their time wisely. While the following record-keeping suggestions serve the purpose of simplifying the verification of tax write-offs or deductions, they also provide an effective means for organizing one's business. Just fifteen minutes a day can result in significant business and tax benefits.

There are a few things that I would strongly suggest that every distributor do, in terms of general record keeping . . .

Establish a Separate Bank Account for the Business.

This is necessary so that a close watch can be kept over both expenditures and income. It will also facilitate easy review for tax purposes. In this regard, I would strongly

107

suggest that a distributor consider adopting a "one write" accounting system. With this technique, as a business check is written, the check's carbon or duplicating surface will imprint the notations on column paper. Each column, in turn, can represent a certain expense, such as travel, entertainment, office, and so on. At the end of each week or month, expenses in each area can be totaled. Such a system is, therefore, a convenient way of keeping track of various expenses with a single notation. This permits one to write the check information only once, thereby lessening the chance that individual records will be lost because they are kept in many places.

Keep a Daily Planner or Calendar.

A distributor should keep track of all appointments, contacts, phone calls, trips, and other business-related items. Normally, a printed daily planner or calendar also includes a place for keeping a log of mileage. It is fairly convenient to keep all mileage records in the planner, and this will keep them up to date on a daily basis. It may be a little difficult to develop the habit of registering each contact or trip, but in time it will become second nature. The use of such a calendar will also help to structure the allocation of one's time. As distributors become increasingly successful, demands on their time become more intense, and calendaring future as well as present events becomes a necessity.

Maintain a Daily Journal.

In many ways, this suggestion may be the best organizational device available to a distributor. Based on my observations, it is also the most underutilized business practice. Such a journal should be updated after each business day—to summarize that day's activities and to plan for the future.

An effective business journal—as discussed in chapter 7—should include entries covering: (1) daily, weekly, monthly, and even yearly goals; (2) actual business contacts, expenses, and efforts made in furtherance of those goals; and (3) a brief but reflective summary of each day's activities in light of those goals. I believe goal setting on a daily, weekly, monthly, and yearly basis is essential in developing an effective multilevel business. Since multilevel business growth is incremental ("line upon line"), unless realistic planning and goal setting occur on a regular basis, a distributor is just "spinning his/her wheels." Many new distributors get involved in a multilevel business and plan or dream on a two- or five-year basis, but fail to connect their dreams and long-range goals with the short-range planning and subgoals that are necessary if those plans are to become a reality. (Goal setting is discussed more specifically in chapter 7.)

The daily journal, which may be kept in an inexpensive three-ring binder or similar device, should include an accounting of all business efforts made in furtherance of one's goals. As previously mentioned, one way to do this is simply to write down the daily goals the night before or on the morning of the day they are to be achieved—and then cross them off after they have been accomplished. When handled in this manner, the business never gets away from a distributor, and he or she gains an increased sense of the controlled growth that accompanies daily planning followed by implementation. Certainly, there can and should be some flexibility in the planning, but too much flexibility can become chaos if it is not part of a larger planned program or system. Of course, one of the great benefits of legitimate multilevel marketing is the willingness of already-successful distributors to help other committed distributors plan their efforts in a systematic and effective manner.

The third facet of a typical journal entry is a brief but reflective analysis of the day's activities. Many people seem to do things rather instinctively. Again, there is a role for spontaneity, but when impulsive behavior dominates, confusion prevails. Taking a few minutes to reflect on specific activities can be enlightening. Asking why a certain contact or goal was or was not achieved during the day can help a distributor to face the problems, both personal and otherwise, that can be expected to arise on a regular basis in operating any business. By promptly facing a problem, the distributor is much more likely to conquer it before it becomes a block to further business growth.

With an accounting system, a calendar, and a journal in hand, a distributor should be able to substantiate virtually any legitimate tax deduction or write-off.

A few specific comments are in order. Just as meticulous records of each contact should be kept, so, too, should documentation exist for each expense related to the business. These records should include the date and time an expense was incurred, the amount of the expenditure, the name and address of the place where the expense occurred, a summary of the reason for the outlay, and the name and relationship of the person for whom the expenditure was made or its business purpose. Obviously, almost all necessary substantiating information can be included in the daily journal. Additionally, where possible, receipts or other proof of each expense or deductible item should be included. One way to do this would be to include with the journal an envelope or series of envelopes in which to place the receipts.

Some people advocate what they call the "bigger shoe box method" for documenting expenses for tax purposes. They believe that the more extensive is one's "shoe box" of records, the less likely is the IRS to push an audit in all areas. While I would agree that complete record keeping is a necessity for business as well as tax purposes, I do not espouse the underlying assumption, which implies a file overflowing with records. I believe a distributor would be far better off to have each expense documented in an organized manner. Rather than planning to overwhelm an IRS agent with a chaotic mass of materials, a taxpayer should simply have in hand clearly documented materials substantiating the business purpose for each expense. If one has an organized business that can produce legitimate tax deductions, there is nothing to fear from an audit. Therefore, an organized operational system not only enables a distributor to increase the likelihood of growth in the business, it also alleviates the need to fear a tax audit.

It should now be clear how the tax savings discussed in the previous chapter can be substantiated. The time required to document one's time and effort is really relatively minimal, if it is done daily so that good habits are formed. It may not be convenient or easy at first, but based on its sheer capacity to increase productivity, keeping such detailed records should become a valued and essential part of every business day.

It would be appropriate to reiterate the major points raised in the last two chapters. I trust that I have made clear my view that operating in multilevel marketing in a businesslike manner not only increases the likelihood of profitability, it also facilitates documentation of legitimate tax-deductible expenses. Multilevel marketing can provide an attractive vehicle for building significant income when operated in a businesslike manner. It will also yield certain tax deductions in the process, but it should never be viewed as a "tax shelter."

10

The Amway Experience

It would be impossible to cover the Amway experience in the limited space of a single chapter. Charles Paul Conn, an author and psychologist with a favorable view of the Amway operation, has examined the human side of Amway in his books, *The Possible Dream*, *The Winner's Circle*, and *An Uncommon Freedom*. Given his extensive treatment of this aspect of the Amway experience, I will largely limit my discussion to the business features of the Amway opportunity.

I will briefly examine both the historical growth of Amway and its future potential as a business. It is impossible, however, to trace the development of the business without also touching on the people who have made Amway a thriving organization in just twenty-five years. In this regard, I will particularly examine the influence of Jay Van Andel and Rich DeVos, the co-founders of Amway.

Jay Van Andel and Rich DeVos became close friends during high school in Grand Rapids, Michigan. They were both enterprising young men who from the beginning were believers in the American Dream. Their friendship was interrupted by World War II, during which they both served in the air force. When they returned home to Michigan after the war, they renewed their friendship.

One of their first cooperative efforts was a near-fulfillment of a dream they had both shared for some time—a sailing adventure. They purchased an old thirty-eight-foot schooner and set sail for the Caribbean and South America, but three months later the schooner sprung a leak and sank off the coast of Cuba. Despite the loss of their schooner, Rich and Jay decided to continue their adventure and traveled throughout Central and South America for a number of months before returning to Grand Rapids and more serious matters.

Upon their return, Rich and Jay eventually formed a direct-selling partnership in the latter part of 1949, as distributors of Nutrilite food supplements. With much hard work and many late nights on the back roads of Michigan, Rich and Jay personally developed a very successful distributorship. They eventually formed Ja-Ri Corporation, which included a sales organization of over 2,000 distributors, many of whom they had personally sponsored or trained.

In 1959, despite the successes of Van Andel and DeVos, their supplier, Nutrilite, was in danger of collapsing, and it was necessary for Rich and Jay to ensure that their sales organization remain viable. Therefore, after some soul-searching, Rich and Jay decided to go into business for themselves. In doing so, they determined to look for products that were readily consumable, relatively low-priced, different from those traditionally found in retail stores, and which would lead to the repeat sales necessary to sustain their strong and growing sales organization.

Before they began to market any products, DeVos and Van Andel had to use care in dealing with the distributors they had sponsored into the Nutrilite business. To that end, they formed an organization of distributors called the American Way Association, the name of which was later changed to the Amway Distributors Association. The primary purpose of this organization was to allow Rich and Jay to communicate with the distributors in the Ja-Ri organization and to keep that organization together until they could develop their own manufacturing and distribution operations.

Given the allegiance of their distributors to the Nutrilite food-supplement business, Rich and Jay proceeded with great caution. Since the distributors were independent, Rich and Jay recognized that some might quit, leaving them with the task of rebuilding a distribution network. It was therefore necessary to have the distributors' cooperation. To do this, Rich and Jay discussed their plans at length with the distributors, including the nature of the proposed product line. As usual, their ideas and their commitment were attractive to the distributors, and many of them joined the American Way Association and began distributing products sold to them by Amway, in addition to Nutrilite products.

By November 1959, Rich and Jay had fully organized Amway Sales Corporation and Amway Services Corporation, and in November 1963, the name of Ja-Ri Corporation was changed to Amway Corporation. In turn, on January 1, 1964, Amway Sales Corporation, Amway Service Corporation, and Amway Manufacturing Corporation merged to form Amway. As a point of interest, it should be noted that in 1972, Amway purchased a 51 percent interest in Nutrilite, and in 1978, purchased additional shares, increasing their share of the Nutrilite business to 89 percent.

In 1959, Amway began with a single product, Frisk—or LOC, as it is known today. Initially, LOC was manufactured by Eckle Company, a small supplier in Detroit, Michigan, and it was one of the few biodegradable liquid detergents available on the market at that time. Shortly thereafter, Ja-Ri Corporation, Amway's predecessor, acquired Eckle Company and moved its assets to Ada, Michigan. A second product was soon added, SA-8, also a biodegradable detergent. With these two innovative products, both of which are still very popular today, Amway had the foundation necessary to begin building the kind of business that the co-founders had envisioned.

That first year, Amway operated out of a small converted gas station, but growth, in terms of physical plant, came very quickly. From that fairly inauspicious beginning, Amway's facility in Ada has expanded to more than 6,800,000 square feet of office, manufacturing, research, distribution, and other business-related space, stretching for nearly one mile across the Michigan countryside. Worldwide, Amway's owned or leased building space today exceeds 7,500,000 square feet.

Of course, the reason for the expansion is obvious—the Amway idea of selling readily consumable, relatively low-priced but high-quality products through a lucrative multilevel marketing system was quickly accepted by the public. With this ever-expanding acceptance, Amway's retail sales grew at a phenomenal rate. In 1959, estimated retail sales totaled $500 thousand. By 1978, revenue reached $500 million, and by 1983, consolidated revenues for Amway had more than doubled to $1.13 billion. Perhaps more importantly, during 1982 alone, Amway paid its distributors over $250 million in bonuses. Sales and bonuses have both grown in an almost geometric fashion since Amway's modest beginning just twenty-five years ago.

To get a real picture of Amway's growth and its potential for future expansion, however, it is necessary to look beyond the figures that represent the corporation's growing retail sales. Amway's product and market development have always been a step or two ahead of retail sales, another reason for the spiraling growth of the business. From two products in 1959, Amway has expanded to the point where a distributor has hundreds of different products to sell. For example, during 1982, Amway added nearly forty new products, and this figure does not include additions to Amway's catalog or personal shoppers' service. Amway now offers a line in five different merchandising areas: home care, personal care, nutrition, houseware and commercial, and personal shopping.

The personalized shopping service features thousands of name-brand products which Amway inventories for its distributors. It also includes handsome gift albums (Amagifts) filled with quality products from which recipients make their own selections. Each day, Amway processes over 40,000 orders from this personalized service.

Amway also sells laundry, dishwashing, floor care, car care, and general-purpose cleaning products in large economical sizes for small commercial businesses in its housewares and commercial division.

It also provides specialized products for the agricultural market. Most importantly, in terms of sales, Amway offers over fifty quality home-care products in nine different groups.

These daily-use products continue to be immensely popular and have consistently accounted for the largest percentage of Amway's sales volume. In another category, Amway offers an array of high-quality housewares products. And in yet another area, Amway offers such nutritional items as vitamins and supplements, as well as nutritious food products, largely produced by Nutrilite. In a final category, Amway produces a complete line of cosmetics and skin-care products and more than fifty other products for personal care. Sales in the latter area alone have risen over 100 percent during the past five years, and Amway completed a new cosmetic manufacturing facility at Ada in 1983, at a cost of $11 million.

For product development, Amway has invested extensively in research to maintain a high level of quality control over its product line. With its 100 percent guarantee (consumers may return any item with which they are not fully satisfied, receiving a full refund for the purchase) and its reputation for quality, Amway is understandably very careful to maintain and develop high product standards. Amway has also been very conscious of maintaining its price structure so that its distributor sales force is able to meet the competition of other product lines in the marketplace.

A few remarks should be made about research and development and pricing. In 1981, Amway opened ultra-modern research facilities, costing approximately $10 million. Amway employs over 250 scientists, technicians, and other staff to work at developing new and better products, improving existing lines, and investigating new ideas. Thus, in 1982, Amway's research and development staff analyzed over 425,000 bits of information, as a result of product-evaluation panel tests on some 32,000 new samples. Amway recognizes that growth demands attention to development and maintenance of a reputation for high-quality products.

Equal attention to pricing has enabled Amway to maintain a high level of customer acceptance for its products. The independent administrative-law judge in the Amway case before the FTC, previously discussed at length, noted that Amway's products were competitively priced. Amway's commitment to quality is matched by its competitive pricing. It recognizes that distributors must be able to sell at competitive prices to maintain their market month after month.

Before turning to consumer acceptance of Amway's products, it should be pointed out that Amway ceased setting retail prices long before the previously mentioned FTC case was initiated in 1975. Retail pricing is now only "suggested," and some distributors sell their products at below the suggested price. While such distributor pricing makes Amway products even more competitive, studies have established that distributors who sell at the suggested retail price actually make more sales than do those selling below that price. In my view, the explanation is simple: Distributors make more money (normally between 30 percent and 40 percent on sales made at the suggested retail price) than when they cut their prices. These profits, in addition to bonuses and overrides, act as an incentive to the distributor and his "downline" to make more sales. Since Amway products are already priced competitively at the suggested retail price—and given consumer satisfaction with the products—I believe that a distributor is foolish in a business sense to sell at below the suggested price, unless he or she wants to give a purchaser a special price for some nonbusiness-related reason.

In addition to prudent product development and competitive pricing, Amway has built its success on a foundation of customer satisfaction and acceptance of its products. In this regard, the administrative-law judge in the Amway case found that:

> Amway's products have very high consumer acceptance. A market study in the record shows that of 37 brands of laundry detergent, Amway's product, with only a very small market share and no national advertising, was third

in brand loyalty. Amway's dishwashing liquid soap led all 16 brands surveyed in consumer acceptance. In each of the markets for automatic dishwasher detergents, detergents for fine clothing, bleaches, rug cleaners, and laundry additives, Amway's products were second in brand loyalty.

The judge then quoted Professor Cady, a marketing specialist from the Harvard Graduate School of Business Administration, as having testified: "What this means overall is that consumers are obviously well served by the products that Amway supplies them with. In fact, they are so well served, in face of a large number of available substitutes, they purchase Amway products to a degree which is almost unknown to other brands in the market."

A more recent independent research study revealed that 84 percent of the customers contacted by Amway distributors buy products at least once, and 53 percent of those customers purchase products every time they are contacted. Furthermore, that same study indicated that two out of every three customers of Amway rate the products as "excellent." This kind of customer approval has contributed to Amway's phenomenal growth, and Amway is clearly committed to retaining that high level of approval.

Amway's overall commitment has enabled the corporation to make significant inroads in the soap and detergents market. According to the judge in the Amway case, Procter & Gamble, the leader in this market, has typically resisted the introduction of each new competitive product by mounting an increased promotional and advertising campaign or by introducing a new product of its own. In doing so, Procter & Gamble has succeeded in monopolizing a great deal of the shelf space in markets where such products are normally sold. Without grocery space and extensive advertising, a new product has little chance for success. Noting these factors, the judge in the Amway case seemingly marveled at Amway's ability to become a force in the soap and detergent marketplace, in which there has been "virtually no new successful entry in the national market for sales of soap and detergents through retail stores in the last thirty years."

The major companies in the soap and detergents area have been able to keep many new businesses out of the market. However, some, like Amway, were able to enter that market by offering innovative and high-quality products, including biodegradable detergents, at competitive prices. Amway, in particular, was aided in its efforts to compete with the "big guys" by virtue of the commitment of its sales force.

In fact, Amway has grown so quickly that many would-be distributors rationalize that it is too late to get into Amway today. They argue that Amway is no longer a ground-floor opportunity. In a humorous sense, Rich DeVos has countered this rationalization by noting that *every* new distributor starts on the ground floor, at the bottom.

Of course, Rich is right. All new distributors start at the bottom, building their own business with training and help from a sponsor and the corporation. The rate and direction of growth for distributors belie the ground-floor myth.

Month after month, the ranks of successful Amway distributors swell. For example, in July 1983 alone, well over 100 newly qualified Directs were noted in Amway's magazine, the *Amagram*. Each direct distributorship represents monthly retail sales of $13,000 or more—with potential gross incomes of approximately $1,000 per month. Each month the story is repeated often with increasing regularity. In fact, in 1982, Amway reported that over 109 distributorships moved up to the higher award levels of Diamond, Double Diamond, Triple Diamond, Crown, and Crown Ambassador, which generally represent incomes from $75,000 or more, per year. Additionally, the ranks of new Directs, Voting Member Directs, Ruby, Pearl, and Emerald Directs were increased by thousands in that same year. Those levels generally represent gross yearly incomes from $10,000 to well over $100,000 per year. The Amway track record proves that there is still plenty of room at the top! Amway's growth rate in every year and at every level and in every area has been characterized by increasing rather than decreasing success.

This should not be surprising for a business that had only about 300,000 distributors in 1975, but has nearly one million today. Furthermore, as the judge in the Amway case noted, there is no persuasive evidence of saturation. (See chapter 4.) Of course, sponsoring in a multilevel business has never been particularly easy, despite great product and business advances in organizations such as Amway and Shaklee.

Not everyone listens and of those who do, not everyone gets involved—but many do and many more will do so in the future. The opportunity is just too good for some to resist, and they are willing to start at the bottom so long as they know they can grow in the business—and they can.

To ensure that the availability of new distributorships will continue unabated, in addition to developing new and improved products, Amway has recently taken some very exciting steps to assist new distributors.

During the past few years, Amway has improved business aids to the point that they are now very professional. The corporation has expanded into modern communications areas and has just recently added a spacious studio to their facilities for the purpose of producing audiovisual, cassette, video, and other support materials for distributors. Through these media and product newsletters and brochures, Amway has developed a comprehensive, coordinated program to help new distributors merchandise their products and build their organizations. Moreover, with the purchase of the Mutual Broadcasting System, Amway is turning to MultiComm, which uses satellite technology to broadcast timely information into the homes of its distributors. Both the corporation and sales organizations within Amway have also turned to computer technology to provide new distributors with late-breaking news, meeting updates (and related sponsorship information that permits distributors to sponsor at a distance), and other pertinent business information. Although a distributor must still sponsor, he or she has all the business aids necessary to make that job as straightforward and simple as possible.

Amway has also assisted its distributors in sponsoring activities by mounting a national advertising campaign aimed at encouraging the public to "get the whole picture." Bob Hope has become Amway's spokesman for this purpose. These ads appear on such programs as ABC-TV's "Good Morning, America," "World News Tonight," and "Nightline." The corporation has also recently launched a nationwide newspaper campaign designed to present "Today's Amway—Better Than Ever" and to overcome the "Amway—Oh, I know all about it" attitude of some prospects. This campaign has covered the fifty states and appeared in newspapers with a readership in excess of 25 million.

Amway has also gone international in a big way. Currently, Amway is conducting business in more than forty nations and territories, ranging from Taiwan to Switzerland. Growth in some of these countries has recently expanded at a rate in excess of 100 percent per year.

For example, in 1962, Amway commenced its Canadian operations and, in 1964, moved into a 4,000-square-foot building in London, Ontario. Since then, Amway of Canada, Ltd., has grown dramatically as the needs of its Canadian distributors have increased. The corporation now occupies some 235,000 square feet of office and warehouse space on an eighty-acre site in London, Ontario, and at Calgary, Alberta.

In 1981, more than eleven million pounds of liquid products and five million pounds of support literature flowed out of the Amway Manufacturing Co., Ltd., in Canada. This corporate success has been matched by successes within the ranks of its distributors in Canada. There are now approximately 100,000 independent Amway distributors in Canada.

All has not been pleasant for Amway's Canadian operation, however. In November 1983, Amway Corporation and Amway of Canada Ltd. agreed to pay a $25 million fine in a criminal action pending against the corporation in Canada. Coincident with this, the criminal actions pending against Rich DeVos, Jay Van Andel, and two other corporate officials, were withdrawn. This action created quite a stir in American and Canadian media and deserves some attention in this book.

Prior to 1965, Amway operated in Canada based on a clear-cut arrangement under Canadian trade and tariff laws. In 1965, however, with a merger between two companies, there was some threat that Amway's tariff rate would be adjusted substantially upward. In an effort to clarify matters, two American officials met with two Canadian tariff officials in 1965. Evidently both sides walked away from that meeting with a different understanding of what had ensued—and, unfortunately for all concerned, the parties failed to reduce the agreement reached at that meeting into proper written form.

Amway, for its part, relied on the understanding of its representatives at the meeting, and it was not until the late 1970s that either Rich DeVos or Jay Van Andel became aware of the fact that there might be a problem with regard to their understanding. When they finally realized this, they obtained legal opinions from attorneys inside and outside of the corporation. Legal counsel agreed that Amway had acted within its rights in adhering to its understanding of what had transpired during the 1965 meeting. It is not surprising that DeVos and Van Andel relied on their attorneys' advice. As an attorney, I fully expect that my clients will take my professional counsel. Unfortunately, as sometimes happens on close legal issues, it appears that Rich and Jay may have received inadequate advice. At any rate, it became clear that the Canadian officials involved were not about to relent in their effort to enforce their understanding of the agreement and to punish Amway for its actions relative to that agreement.

While the corporation would be liable for the acts of its agents, it should be emphasized that Rich and Jay never acknowledged any criminal activity on their part. In fact, they both have consistently denied that they participated in any fraudulent or illegal acts. Although it is possible that the corporation, through its agents, acted in an improper fashion, that does not in and of itself establish wrongdoing on the part of DeVos and Van Andel.

Ultimately, however, it became clear to DeVos and Van Andel that to continue to litigate the matter for the purpose of proving that they were not personally involved in any improper activity would have resulted in legal costs conservatively estimated at $30–$40 million over a ten-year period, and would have been a source of continuing trauma for their Canadian distributors. As a matter of practical business judgment, therefore, Rich and Jay opted to get the situation behind them and their distributors by agreeing to have Amway Corporation and Amway of Canada Ltd. pay the fine, despite the fact that they continued to receive legal advice from their attorneys to the effect that they did not need to settle the matter. As a lawyer, it is certainly conceivable to me that DeVos and Van Andel realized that nothing could be gained, in a business sense, from proceeding to trial.

Settlement of the type reached in the Canadian criminal action in no way proves guilt or improper activity on the part of either Rich DeVos or Jay Van Andel, or on the part of any corporate official. It was unfortunate for all concerned that the matter had to be resolved in the manner that it was. However, it was clearly sound business judgment to favor continuing to engage in the work Amway has excelled at, rather than putting more and more dollars into legal battle that would ultimately cost more to defend than the actual $25 million settlement, and that would continue to hinder the growth of the Amway business in Canada.

Before returning to the role of both DeVos and Van Andel in building the business, a few additional developments should be noted, because they illustrate the growth and maturity of the Amway operation. Amway has enjoyed successes in other areas, as well. The corporation purchased the Mutual Broadcasting System in 1978, and under Amway's leadership, it has grown to include over 950 radio stations and, as previously noted, recently initiated use of a ten-million-dollar satellite system. Amway also recently completed the first phase in its development of a sixty-four-million-dollar hotel project in downtown

Grand Rapids. This project is also indicative of the commitment of Jay Van Andel and Rich DeVos to building a better America. Prior to undertaking the hotel project, Amway had purchased the Peter Island Yacht Club and Resort in the British Virgin Islands. This 500-acre resort has been dubbed "one of the most glamorous anchorages in the world" by *Motor Boating and Sailing* magazine. Amway's use of both the resort and the corporate yachts to reward its distributors also illustrates Amway's commitment to the American free-enterprise system of incentives for production.

With all these developments, Amway has grown to be the second-largest direct-sales business in the world, and it is among the 275 largest industrial corporations in the United States. With its continuing growth, Amway may overtake Avon, the largest direct-sales business. It should be noted that Avon is not a multilevel business, although there is some talk of Avon's going in that direction.

All this success sprang from the commitment of Amway's co-founders, Rich DeVos and Jay Van Andel, and the willingness of nearly one million distributors to share in their dreams, thereby reaching for some of their own. There is a certain chemistry between Rich and Jay that has been present since they first met in high school. Rich is dynamic and has the ability to stimulate Amway's distributor force. Jay, in turn, is a respected and immensely able administrator. In light of their involvement in politics, this chemistry had led some people to jest that Rich has said that he will run for the United States presidency if Jay will serve—and Jay has responded that he will serve if Rich will run. They have both brought to their friendship—and ultimately to the Amway business—a complementary store of talents.

Jay Van Andel is chairman of the board of Amway

Corporation and other Amway companies around the world. He is also a director and past chairman of the board of the United States Chamber of Commerce. His business and administrative abilities have been recognized in other contexts as well. He has served or is now serving as: director and founding chairman of Citizen's Choice; trustee of Hillsdale College; member of the Japan/United States Council on Economic Relations; the United States national chairman of the Netherlands/American Bicentennial Committee; and director of the Hudson Institute of Research in New York City. He has also been honored as a member of Omicron Delta Kappa National Honor Society, has received the distinguished service award of the Rotary Club, the Religious Heritage Foundation's "Great Living American Award," and holds three honorary doctorates from state universities. This tally of accomplishments is far short of the kind of list that should properly be used to portray Jay Van Andel's many talents and his willingness to serve, at the community, state, national, and international levels.

Rich DeVos, in turn, is equally talented, although his abilities often shine in different areas. He is president of Amway Corporation and other Amway companies around the world. He has also served as the chairman of the National Republican Leadership Council, has been past chairman of the Direct Selling Association of the United States, and is chairman of the board of Gospel Films, Inc. As with Jay Van Andel, the list of his accolades and accomplishments is simply too long to detail here.

Rich has authored a book, *I Believe*, that I would recommend as inspirational and enlightening reading. He has also been repeatedly honored for his service. His contributions were ably summarized in a recent article in the *Saturday Evening Post*, in which the author stated that "Rich has a trunkful of service awards as well as honorary doctorates. But perhaps as indicative of his clout as any is the 'Excellence in Management' Award given by *Industry Week*, the prestigious business magazine that selected him over such finalists as the chairman of U.S. Steel and the chairman of Mobil Oil. The award characterized him as a 'business philosopher who has mastered the art of communication. . . .'"

In addition to their respective talents and charisma, DeVos and Van Andel have offered another ingredient which has helped make the Amway business what it is today. They have added a sense of mission. Noel Black, a former employee of Amway, perhaps put it best when he quoted Rich DeVos as having said, "Noel, no business will prosper unless it has a mission larger than itself. You can't merely manufacture 'widgets' and expect that by itself to be rewarding. There must be a cause; and the cause we have in our business is the preservation of free enterprise and individual freedom. . . ." Certainly, there are those who would disparage Rich DeVos for holding to such a lofty purpose for a "mere soap business," just as there are those who are inclined to dismiss the free-enterprise system itself, but it would be difficult for anyone to doubt that both Rich and Jay believe in the mission of the Amway business. This belief, in turn, has stimulated a similar commitment on the part of many of Amway's distributors, and has provided them with a business and a mission of their own.

Lest the reader be left with the impression that Amway is just another soap company successfully engaged in door-to-door selling, it will be helpful to describe briefly how and why the Amway business works. My presentation is necessarily sketchy. For the "whole picture," I would recommend that the reader talk with an active and successful Amway distributor.

Direct sales, as practiced today by legitimate multilevel marketing businesses, rarely emphasizes a door-to-door approach. As practiced in Amway, Shaklee, and other legitimate multilevel businesses, direct sales of product are typically made to people known to the distributor. The emphasis is placed on serving a limited number of customers well and on developing a business organization by sponsoring other distributors into the business. The selling theme in both Amway and Shaklee focuses on a professional approach based on proven methods designed to embrace customer service and the efficient management of one's business. While permitted, door-to-door selling is certainly the exception to the rule, because it has proven to be a much less successful means of building one's business than the professional approach emphasizing customer service and organizational development. As I have noted throughout this chapter, Amway has built and is continuing to build an image of permanence and respectability.

This has been accomplished primarily because Amway has sold excellent products t ough a multilevel system that rewards production anc performance. That system includes a series of performance bonuses or overrides, based on sales and payable to Amway's distributor force.

The performance bonuses are paid, in the first instance, by Amway to the Direct Distributors (those who have a monthly point value of 7,500—about $13,000 at retail—and who deal directly with the corporation). Each Direct is then responsible for paying out performance bonuses, from the amount received from Amway, to the second-level distributors he or she personally sponsored. They, in turn, pay their "downline," and the process continues down to the newest distributor.

A Direct Distributor will pay out less than what was received from Amway—because the second-level distributors will have a lower point value and will therefore receive a lower percentage of the amounts of their respective business volumes. For example, if five second-level distributors had each purchased a large enough volume of products in a month to be entitled to a 15 percent performance bonus, the Direct Distributor would be paid by Amway twenty-five cents on every dollar of his/her volume—but would pay out only an average of fifteen cents to second-level distributors on each dollar of *their* respective business volumes. Thus, Direct Distributors receive a portion of a twenty-five-cent bonus on each dollar of volume in their entire group, in addition to the 20–40 percent markup on the retail sales. In turn, each of the "downline" distributors make not only their regular sales commission but a performance bonus paid to them by their sponsor on their qualifying sales.

Each second-level distributor is then responsible for paying out performance bonuses (from the amount received from the Direct Distributor) to the third-level distributors he or she sponsored. Second-level distributors will make money on business volume generated by their sponsored distributors in the same way the Direct Distributors made money on the volume of the second-level distributors—and so on down the successive levels of distributors. Typically, when the commission on the retail sales and the bonus are combined, a distributor selling a given product will make more money from the sale than will his or her sponsor.

Furthermore, in the words of Commissioner Pitofsky,

who wrote the opinion for the Federal Trade Commission in the Amway case: "This distribution hierarchy is not static, however, as any regular distributor, regardless of how many levels he may be below his Direct Distributor, may himself become a Direct Distributor by reaching a specified high volume of purchases three months in a row. When a regular distributor qualifies as a Direct Distributor, he breaks out of the field of sponsorship he was in up to that time and begins to make his wholesale purchases directly from Amway. When a new Direct Distributor breaks out of his old non-Direct position like this, he takes with him all those distributors he sponsored, all the distributors those persons sponsored, etc." In turn, the Direct Distributor's sponsor receives a bonus on the sales of the new Direct Distributor and his or her group. That override or bonus is normally 3 percent.

As the production of one's "downline" increases, the percentage received by a successful sponsor may go down, but the profits for all concerned go up. This, in turn, helps to stimulate training of one's "downline" and facilitates growth in their productivity by providing a strong incentive system.

Obviously, it is very difficult to explain the Amway marketing and compensation system in a brief excerpt. Therefore, I would reiterate that someone should hear the specifics of the Amway compensation plan firsthand from an active distributor or his or her sponsor. For our present purposes, it will suffice to say that the plan is structured to compensate distributors according to their (and their group's) production, and it compensates that production very well. In fact, it has provided a means to economic independence for thousands of distributors.

Rich DeVos summed up the essence of the Amway

experience and the attitude of most successful distributors when he stated:

> This is an exciting world. It is crampacked with opportunity. Great moments await around every corner. It is a world that deserves an upward look. We have heard enough from the critics, the nay-sayers, the cynics whose vocabularies have not progressed beyond the word "no," the rip artists whose talents of seeing sore spots have made instant experts and heroes of them. I believe in life with a large "yes" and a small "no." I believe that life is good, that people are good, that God is good. And I believe in affirming every day that I live, proudly and enthusiastically, that life in America under God is a positive experience.*

That's Amway! It's a way in which many people have been able to make their material dreams a reality—but it is also much, much more. It is Rich DeVos, Jay Van Andel and over one million distributors who believe that life is a positive experience—and who are all busily engaged in doing their part to ensure that Amway will always be a positive way to achieve one's economic dreams and aspirations.

---

*From "Faith and Family," by Fred Birmingham, *Saturday Evening Post,* July/Aug. 1983, p. 116. Used with permission of The Saturday Evening Post Society, a division of BFL & MS, Inc. © 1983.

11

The Shaklee Opportunity

As was the case in the preceding chapter which dealt with the Amway experience, I will largely limit my discussion here to the development of the Shaklee business and its future business potential.

Again, there are books on the market that deal with the philosophical and the human side of the Shaklee business. In this regard, I would recommend Robert L. Shook's *The Shaklee Story*, which chronicles both the historical development and the human side of this business. Additionally, *Reflections on a Philosophy*, by Forrest C. Shaklee, Sr., contains a collection of essays on his philosophy of "thoughtsmanship," and George Spunt's book, *When Nature Speaks*, is a biography of Dr. Shaklee.

Since these books are already available, I generally feel secure in dwelling principally on the business aspects of the organization. As with Amway, one cannot strictly separate the development of the Shaklee business from the personality, charisma, and vision of its founder, Forrest C. Shaklee, Sr., and his sons. Their effort, ingenuity, commitment—and their belief in maintaining "harmony with nature"—turned a good idea into one of America's largest corporations in just twenty-five years.

This did not come quickly or easily for Forrest Shaklee, Sr. Despite the fact that he had believed since boyhood in good health through proper nutrition and physical exercise, Forrest Shaklee and his sons did not start the Shaklee business until he was sixty years old. At that time he had already enjoyed successes in many areas. He was a successful chiropractor, a published author and philosopher, an inventor and researcher, and had even been successful as a radio pastor. Forrest Shaklee, Sr., could have retired as a successful man at sixty, but he had maintained the vigor of his youth and simply could not quit. Instead, he began the greatest adventure of his life and lived that idea day in and day out until he was in his 80s.

In 1955, Dr. Shaklee, who had always been interested in nutritional research, particularly that dealing with vitamins, had an idea. As is so often the case in good parent-child relationships, Forrest wanted to share this idea with his sons, Forrest, Jr., who was an accountant, and Lee, who was already successful in insurance sales. The idea was simple—Shaklee felt that he had benefited from his own consumption of vitamins and food supplements and wanted to share this secret of good health with others.

The idea was interesting to both sons, who had great faith in their father and his idea. For the next six months, they thought about how they could best ensure that their idea could reach the maximum number of people.

They finally decided on the direct-sales approach, because it would permit them to teach others some of the benefits of selected nutritional items on a one-to-one basis, hoping that those people, in turn, would share the idea with still others. Multilevel marketing was a natural for them—it would permit them to get started without an enormous investment and would enable them to reach a broad audience. Since vitamins and food supplements were almost an unknown quantity in the era of the 1950s, they had to educate the consumer. Through multilevel marketing, the Shaklees could teach one distributor who, in turn, could teach another. Their idea could thus be duplicated time and again. Furthermore, the multilevel marketing plan squared with the Shaklees' belief that people ought to live by the Golden Rule, doing unto others as they would have them do unto themselves. The business and the basic idea could only succeed if people practiced the Golden Rule in its most positive sense—when they helped someone else to become more successful, they would join in that person's successes.

With this in mind, and with a compensation plan developed by Lee, Shaklee began operation on April 1, 1956, with a minimal financial investment and a tremendous time commitment on the part of the three Shaklees. They had each contributed $6,000 and had left their own respective, successful businesses with a genuine commitment to make their idea a personal as well as an economic success.

In that first year, the Shaklees did approximately $100,000 in retail sales. Nevertheless, since they knew they were just beginning, they put most of the money they personally made back into the business. With such financial and personal commitment, the business continued to grow. Thus, by 1973, Shaklees formed a public corporation, offering shares to the public, and by 1979, were listed on the prestigious New York Stock Exchange. In 1973, Shaklee had grown to the point that yearly retail sales were at the $75 million mark—but this was only the beginning. By 1979, there were sales of $314 million, which increased to $500 million by 1982. Shaklee stock was among the very top producers on the New York Stock Exchange and by

1982—its Jubilee or twenty-fifth anniversary—the corporation became one of the Fortune 500, a listing by *Fortune* magazine of the 500 largest publicly owned businesses in the United States.

Listing the statistics does not tell the whole story. In the early years, the Shaklees and their loyal distributors spent endless hours of effort toward building the business. At first, they acted on faith, with works following thereafter. Forrest Shaklee, Sr., referred to their early efforts as "pioneering," but Lee probably most effectively characterized that early period as the "crusading" years. As Lee is quoted in Robert Shook's *The Shaklee Story:* "A crusader picks up his lance and charges onward, no matter what. He has to have strong faith. When he's knocked down he picks himself up and goes forward again. I don't believe an entrepreneur can survive unless he has the crusader's drive." The Shaklees and their early distributors were pioneers, crusaders, and entrepreneurs in every sense of the words.

By 1973, the Shaklees felt that they were ready to take yet another step in the development of their business by becoming a public corporation. As entrepreneurs, they had built a thriving operation, but they believed it was time to move on to corporate management, whereby business affairs would be run by a group of trained professions. The Shaklees would remain on the board of directors, where they could share their ideas and know-how, but they would turn over the day-to-day corporate business decisions to individuals trained to deal with them. This idea, too, proved to be very successful.

From 1974 to 1977, sales tripled—rising from $79 million in 1974 to $242 million in 1977. Sales from 1977 to 1982 more than doubled. Shaklee had become the leader in the direct-sales vitamin and food supplement market and has enjoyed great success on the stock market, indicating what investors think of its status and growth potential. Between January 1982 and May 1983, for example, Shaklee stock skyrocketed from just over $15 per share to over $72 per share, at which level it split. While Shaklee's stock dropped below $20 per share after the split, it has consistently maintained a level or value twice that existing in January, 1982. A share that was valued at $15 in 1982 is worth approximately $40 as of April 1984 when the split is taken into account. In November 1982, Mitchell Gordon did an article for the prestigious investment periodical, *Barrons*, in which he stated that Shaklee was "poised for robust growth," and proceeded to explain why this was the case.

Based on its commitment to professional corporate management and the dedication of its sales leaders and distributors at the marketing level, Shaklee has mapped a four-point strategy for the 1980s. First is a commitment to increased research and development, because of the recognition that phenomenal growth is dependent upon effective product development and quality control. Second is a commitment to expanding and perfecting its manufacturing capability. Third, Shaklee is committed to maintaining its dedication to quality products and competitive pricing, while also expanding its capacity to produce products that are appealing to the consumer. Finally, and perhaps most importantly, Shaklee is committed to its distributors, since the business will only be as strong as the people who market its products. One can best understand the Shaklee business and its future potential by examining each of these four strategies separately.

Early in 1978, Dr. James Scala, who was previously a nutritionist with General Foods, joined Shaklee for the express purpose of strengthening the company's research effort, which at that time was primarily aimed at quality control. Due to Dr. Scala's efforts and management's desire to expand its research and development capability, Shaklee increased funds budgeted for this purpose 300 percent —from $2.4 million in 1978 to approximately $7 million in 1982.

Shaklee now employs more scientists with advanced degrees in pharmacy, nutrition, food science, food technology, chemistry, and microbiology than any of its direct-sales competitors in the nutrition field. By November of 1980, it had more than twice as many research scientists on the payroll as its nearest competitor, General Nutrition Corporation.

Shaklee has also continued exhaustive efforts toward quality control. As many as 262 tests are performed on a single Shaklee product, and sometimes up to 176 quality tests are performed on raw material used by Shaklee. In addition, Shaklee is the only nutrition company that does extensive, independent clinical testing to confirm the effectiveness of its products. For example, in conjunction with the introduction of its diet program, Slim Plan, independent clinical tests were run on the product at Georgetown University's Diet Management Clinic. Before introducing its latest line of personal-care products, Shaklee Natural, the corporation had the line tested clinically to confirm the effectiveness of the products.

By tripling its appropriation for research and development and by its continuing dedication to quality control, Shaklee has positioned itself for significant gains in the 1980s. Each time Shaklee has introduced a major new product, it has enjoyed substantial growth in sales and in its sales force. There is, of course, some lag time between when the expenditure is made for research and development and when the new product is ready for marketing. However, during the past couple of years, Shaklee has spent $6–7 million per year for the development of exciting new products. Shaklee has a significant potential for growth as a result of such new products as Slim Plan and its Natural line of personal-care products and others to be introduced in the future.

In another sense, Shaklee has positioned itself for substantial gains in the eighties by solidifying its manufacturing base. It now owns or leases over two million square feet of manufacturing, warehouse, and office space. Shaklee streamlined its manufacturing capability in 1980 by closing its Hayward, California, facility, which had produced a number of household items. However, the company's commitment to product development and ultramodern manufacturing techniques, particularly in the nutritional area, has placed it in a strong position. New facilities will enhance Shaklee's competitiveness in its most profitable areas. (Nutrition accounts for 75 percent of all sales.)

The $50-million, 250,000-square-foot Forrest C. Shaklee Research Center in Norman, Oklahoma, which became operational in August 1979, represents the single most exciting development in Shaklee's recent history. That facility is larger, better equipped, and better staffed than those of Shaklee's immediate competitors in the nutrition field.

Salomon Brothers' company analysis of May 26, 1981, found Shaklee to be a good investment, based in substantial part on the conclusion: "Profits will benefit from new product momentum and manufacturing economies from the company's new Norman, Oklahoma, plant, which can handle more than double the existing sales volume without having to hire many more employees. In the longer term, Shaklee has the key ingredients for success as a direct-selling company, namely a product in good demand, a highly motivated and well compensated sales force as well as effective strategic planning."

In a more specific sense, that same report indicated that "in 1980 and 1981, Shaklee's margins are expected to expand because of cost economies related to the Norman, Oklahoma, plant. This plant, which began to operate in 100 percent of planned efficiency late in fiscal 1979, can handle triple Shaklee's existing vitamin volume, with nominal expansion of its labor force of 200. Because of the plant's more central location in the U.S., freight costs, which now equal 3–4 percent of sales, will decline."

In that report, Salomon Brothers went on to conclude that the efficiency and capacity of the Norman facility should permit Shaklee to continue to be the "low-cost producer of primarily natural vitamins. . . ." Obviously, the research center in Norman is more than an ultra-modern manufacturing facility—it is a key ingredient in Shaklee's planned future success.

The Norman facility does not stand alone. Shaklee has additional building and manufacturing space of approximately 1,750,000 square feet. Much of this space is allocated to the Fort Worth, Texas, facility where fruit bars are produced, five regional warehouses which make Shaklee products more readily available for distributors, and Shaklee Terraces, a thirty-eight-story office building in San Francisco.

The fruit bars produced in Fort Worth represent one of Shaklee's fairly recent efforts in the snack-food market, which presently represents potential sales of nearly $5 billion per year. The company is preparing to enter that market in a concerted fashion, and is betting on the fact that Americans will combine their desire for good physical health with their demand for snack foods. These factors should support a growing market for the kind of high-quality, reasonably priced nutritional snack foods offered by Shaklee.

The regional warehouses, in turn, represent Shaklee's efforts to strengthen the real key to its success, its sales force. By maintaining these regional facilities, Shaklee helps to ensure that the product line runs consistently from production to the distributors. To aid in this effort, Field Service Centers function as a personal link to the home office for every sales leader in every region. Shaklee has taken these steps to guarantee that a product is always readily available when needed.

Shaklee Terraces is more than just another impressive high-rise in San Francisco's financial district. It is the corporate center for field support services, such as the bonus car program, travel and other incentive plans, and virtually all administrative functions other than research and manufacturing. A facility called the Centerra also exemplifies the Shaklee philosophy of good health and well-being. The Centerra is actually a physical fitness center occupying the third floor of the Shaklee Terraces. In the Centerra, Shaklee employees are encouraged to combine physical exercise with the good nutrition philosophy of Shaklee Corporation.

Although Shaklee has become a public corporation, it still retains its vision that a healthy person is also more productive.

Even extensive research and development, manufacturing, and vision are not enough to make a good business successful. It must also have quality products and good people to distribute them. Shaklee has both of these.

Since Shaklee's quality products are sold at competitive prices, there is a high level of consumer acceptance for them. The products are in three major categories: nutrition (vitamins, supplements, diet aids, food products);

household products (soaps, detergents, cleansers, and so on); and items for personal care such as cosmetics, cleansers, moisturizers, shampoos, and hair conditioners.

All of Shaklee's products go through rigid testing and stringent developmental standards before being placed on the market. Shaklee also prefers to have its products clinically tested, to confirm any representations made regarding the products.

Perhaps Shaklee's product position was best summarized in a recent article in *Advertising Age*. In that article, which dealt with Shaklee's new line of personal-care products, the author made the following statement:

> The products . . . emphasize nature, claiming to use the most natural ingredients available in personal care.
>
> These products represent the best of both worlds. . . . Most products on the market are either very natural, without promising much in the way of end results, or they're very performance oriented, without regard to natural ingredients. This line [Shaklee Natural] will offer quality and will ensure the customer that she is getting the most natural products available.

Shaklee prides itself on quality and harmony with nature in its product lines and takes the precautions necessary to assure that such levels are maintained.

Shaklee's quality products are available at competitive prices. As the 1981 report by Salomon Brothers noted: "Competitively, Shaklee has restrained its price increases since 1977 to compete with such discounters as General Nutrition. . . . As a result of this more competitive pricing strategy of its commodity-oriented items, the introduction of more proprietary products, and the construction of the Norman plant, Shaklee seems well positioned with regard to its competition."

This sensitivity to pricing extends to products other than vitamins. In the *Advertising Age* article discussing Shaklee's new personal-care product line, the author, Betsy Gilbert, emphasized: "In addition to the training aspect, Shaklee has given a great deal of thought to the area of pricing. It is a sensitive issue. It is undeniable that people today are careful about spending their money. When they do decide to make a purchase, they want a lot of value for the dollar. Shaklee takes that into consideration, setting prices that are competitive to both retail products and direct sales products offered by Mary Kay and Avon."

Shaklee seeks to maintain competitive pricing for all of its products without compromising quality. Its prices may not compete with "discounters" in every instance, but Shaklee is certainly competitive with other organizations which are producing similar products at the same general quality level. Furthermore, Shaklee's planned expansion in product development and manufacturing, has enhanced its competitive position. It appears unlikely that Shaklee will relinquish its number-one position in the growing vitamin market, and it apparently will also make inroads in other areas.

This attention to quality and pricing, of course, has contributed to a high level of consumer acceptance for Shaklee's products. Like Amway, Shaklee has an unconditional guarantee on all of its products, which provides for exchange or full refund if a customer is dissatisfied for any reason.

Noting the high degree of consumer acceptance, the Salomon Brothers report concluded: "Among consumers, Shaklee has a reputation for product quality because of its use of natural ingredients. . . . Among many nutrition enthusiasts, Shaklee vitamins have a certain mystique because of their ingredient formulations. While product claims have become more circumscribed in Shaklee's transition from an entrepreneurial company to a professionally managed company, this mystique remains."

Salomon Brothers also noted that sociologically, "Shaklee consumers tend to be highly educated, family oriented, somewhat religious and usually suburban, according to Shaklee's research. Also, their alcohol consumption is low and they watch a minimal amount of TV. Consumption of Shaklee products is frequently accompanied by a change in lifestyle that includes greater emphasis on proper nutrition and increased exercise. Conceptually, that is, Shaklee is selling better nutrition and physical fitness—a lifestyle that attracts Americans today."

Shaklee has enjoyed its successes without advertising on the national level—it depends on word of mouth to spread its message of better health and nutrition. In refraining from widespread advertising, Shaklee has gained the support of its distributors, who believe that limiting the advertising budget increases the pot from which they will be compensated. In her article in *Advertising Age*, Betsy Gilbert noted: "Unlike Mary Kay and Avon, the company does no formal advertising, emphasizing instead sales incentives programs and product development as more constructive uses for its money."

The great source of Shaklee's success, therefore, is the commitment of its sales force. Shaklee has approximately 2,000,000 so-called distributors, although the vast majority of them do not actively try to sponsor and build a business; they simply have signed up to buy Shaklee products at a discount. In fact, 90 percent of Shaklee's product sales are purchases by distributors at wholesale, the other 10 percent being sold at retail.

Distributors who do seek to sponsor and build a sales

organization are well compensated. As was the case with the Amway compensation plan, I cannot explain the Shaklee plan in the detail it deserves. Therefore, I again strongly urge the reader to contact an active Shaklee distributor/sponsor to learn more about the mechanics of the business and the manner of compensation.

Shaklee's plan is also based on the multilevel concept: You sponsor and train others and then receive a bonus based on their sales as well as your own. As with Amway, a distributor can make money through both personal sales and overrides or bonuses.

For each sale at the suggested retail price (there is no fixed price), a distributor normally makes approximately 35 percent commission. If distributors have enough sales or personal purchases in a month, they may also receive an additional override for their sales and a bonus for the sales of distributors in their "downline" sales organization.

From a monthly volume of approximately $100 up to a volume less than $1,000 per month, the bonus is 3–8 percent, which must be shared with "downline" distributors who have also reached bonus levels. When there are sales of approximately $1,000 in a distributor's group, the bonus is 11 percent, and he or she is made an assistant supervisor. The percentage increases until monthly sales or purchases reach approximately $3,500, at which time the distributor becomes a supervisor and is entitled to a bonus of 23 percent, depending on the organization's purchase volume. In turn, when the group has three other distributors who become supervisors, the first-level distributor becomes a coordinator and qualifies for even more bonuses.

Shaklee just recently made some revisions in their bonus structure to help stimulate further growth in its sales leader force and in other sales ranks. These revisions provide an exciting array of new benefits for successful distributors, ranging from additional overrides or bonuses to special incentives for specified growth in individual distributorships. These changes evidence Shaklee Corporation's continuing commitment to stimulating growth among its distributors by providing exciting incentives for achievement. It should be emphasized that the Shaklee compensation plan works very well for many of its distributors as their vehicle to economic well-being.

The success potential is extremely high for those who try to build a business by both sponsoring and selling Shaklee products. According to the Salomon Brothers 1981 report, Shaklee had 10,000 sales leaders or managers at the end of fiscal 1980. The average beginning sales leader earns more than $10,000 in gross income and typical top distributors with one or more leaders under them earn about $14,000. Approximately 5,500 also qualify for a bonus car from the company. Additionally, Shaklee has approximately 1,000 coordinators (those who have developed four or more first-level supervisors) who average about $50,000 in gross income annually. Of that group, approximately 200 make over $100,000 per year in gross income, with some earning over $400,000 per year.

Approximately 40 percent of Shaklee's wholesale price goes toward sales incentives. In 1974, incentives were paid in the sum of $37,200,000, and by 1981, incentives had increased over 450 percent to $171,500,000. In his article, "Healthy Glow: Vitamin Producer Shaklee Poised for Robust Gains," appearing in *Barrons* on November 29, 1982, Mitchell Gordon predicted: "The company should benefit in fiscal 1983 from a larger corps of sales leaders. The big April-May-June recruiting season is still ahead, and coincides with the qualification period for the company's big annual international convention (to be held this year at

Monte Carlo). Shaklee has its sights set on adding at least 1,000 to 1,500 more sales leaders by the end of fiscal 1983. . . ."

Although Shaklee experienced a slight drop in the number of sales leaders in 1982, with the introduction of some exciting new products and the corporation's commitment to adding new leaders, it is not surprising that Salomon Brothers concluded that "the sales force can easily grow 10%–15% a year given its small base," and that "if Shaklee were particularly successful in planning its field operations it could probably achieve 15%–20% growth a year in its sales force with an impressive 20%–25% earnings growth a year." The projected figure becomes impressive when one notes that it would represent 1,000 to 2,000 new sales leaders each year, with gross annual incomes generally in the $10,000-to-$14,000 range. If the figures remain uniform, there would be 100 to 200 new coordinators with gross incomes of approximately $50,000 per year, and 20 to 40 new leaders with gross incomes of $100,000 or more each year.

The corporation appears committed to make that kind of growth a reality. It has produced a vast array of professional business aids, directed at helping distributors build a profitable business. To promote its products, Shaklee has worked hard at establishing a firm, scientific image. Attractive incentives augment the potential income figures noted above. Leading distributors attend Supervisors Conventions, Leadership Conventions, an International Coordinators Convention, and a President's Club Convention. The corporation often pays all or a substantial portion of the expense of such conventions, which are held at fine hotels in exciting places. The bonus car program offers a wide selection of automobiles, from Chevrolets and Buicks to Cadillacs and Lincolns (even Rolls Royces).

The Shaklee Bonus Car Fleet is one of the largest in America, more than 5,500 strong, and is made up of cars leased and insured by Shaklee Corporation for use by its successful sales leaders.

In addition to all of the foregoing, as does Amway, Shaklee offers regional rallies on a regular basis to train and inspire its sales force. These are generally highly motivational meetings that provide information and build belief in the business.

Forrest Shaklee, Sr., and his sons Forrest, Jr. and Lee, started the Shaklee business over twenty-five years ago in the belief that they could help some people to better health and greater economic well-being. The results of their dream undoubtedly surprise even the ever-optimistic Shaklees. Many people have shared the dream, reaping both physical and economic benefits from their participation in the Shaklee business.

In speaking of the corporation, Dr. Shaklee has stated, "You will find us an energetic and optimistic family. We are a group of caring, successful people with an interest in good nutrition, a respect for nature, and a love for people embodied in the Golden Rule." Certainly, not everyone involved in Shaklee shares Forrest Shaklee's optimism or his success, but many do, and many more will in the future. Shaklee is a dynamic, income-generating opportunity—and more. It reaches for the stars of economic well-being and good health, while keeping its feet firmly planted on the ground, basing its future on research and product development and support for its sales force.

12

Selecting the Right Multilevel Business

Once a person decides to get involved in multilevel marketing, he or she should take care in evaluating the many multilevel businesses available. Unfortunately, most new distributors do not give this matter much thought; they simply join the first multilevel business that tickles their fancy. Selecting the right program should not be such an irrational matter, as there are a number of criteria to be examined before choosing a business. Very few people think of buying a new car without looking at most of the competitors. Similarly, it is foolhardy to jump into the first business that appears on the scene. Before getting involved, take a week or two and look at the competition, and then make as rational a decision as you can before getting started.

In a recent article appearing in *Elks Magazine*, the Direct Selling Association suggested four general yardsticks that should be applied in selecting a direct-sales business. They suggest that the would-be distributor carefully examine (1) the product line; (2) the management of the company; (3) the compensation plan; and (4) the company's commitment to quality sales and training assistance. I will examine these four criteria in greater detail, and will illustrate how the two giants of the industry, Amway and Shaklee, meet those criteria.

1. Product Line.

In examining the product line, one must consider the quality of the products, the viability of the market for those products, the price structure, consumer acceptance of the products, and whether there is assurance of an adequate supply of the products being readily available at all times. With their 100 percent unconditional guarantees, their commitment to quality control in terms of dollars and effort, and the high level of consumer acceptance for their products, Amway and Shaklee are both prime examples of companies with good products. Furthermore, since their products are consumed on a regular and repeated basis, they are particularly attractive candidates for multilevel marketing.

In my view, both Amway and Shaklee satisfy the product criteria necessary for the success of any multilevel business. However, there are other, newer marketing organizations that should also be scrutinized by a would-be distributor.

In examining any new program, a prospective distributor should take the time to analyze the company's efforts toward quality control. In this regard, the distributor should first determine whether there is a 100 percent unconditional guarantee and full-refund policy, whether each representation by the company is supported by concrete evidence, and whether there is a high level of consumer acceptance of the product.

The would-be distributor must be wary of unsubstantiated claims about the products. I recently heard of a multilevel business which is marketing herbal products based on "a secret, fifteen-century-old formula." These herbs are represented as cure-alls for everything from cancer to the common cold. Any such claims ought to trigger a red flag on the part of a prospective distributor. Not only could they ultimately subject the company and a distributor to a costly law suit, but it is also likely that the Federal Drug Administration will either restrict the use of the product (and the claims) until extensive testing is done, or it will simply take it off the market. Either result could be fatal to a distributor who has started to build a business based on such lofty representations. Furthermore, in the legal mess that may develop, the new distributor could be left with an inventory of products that the company either cannot or will not buy back. Representations that are "too good to be true" are usually false.

Once the quality of the products is established, a prospective distributor must also determine whether there is a viable market for them. There must be people who would purchase the products offered and continue to do so on a regular basis. I had a friend who began selling computers in a multilevel marketing business which suddenly came upon bad times when the price of computers plummeted. My friend had soon sold all the computers he was able to sell. The sales commission on the computers was good, until the price dropped, but there was no repeat market that would purchase the same product month after month.

The success of Amway and Shaklee has been based on quality products for a market that permits distributors to engage in repeat sales to the same customers. The distributors can then concentrate on widening both their sponsorship and their customer base. I am personally aware of another multilevel company that recently got involved with home-entertainment products. Despite the fact that the products are of high quality, they have had a very difficult time. For example, a customer may buy a tape one week and not buy another for a month or two. The company has not been able to maintain a steady pattern of product sales, on which commissions and bonuses are paid.

Another matter to be analyzed to ascertain market potential is consumer acceptance of the product.

Does the company have a successful track record of maintaining satisfied customers? To determine whether the products are appealing, a prospective distributor should not place much credence on the testimonials of existing distributors, because they obviously have a conflict of interest. What ought to be done is to present the product to a number of people who are not involved with the business, and then ask them if they would purchase the product at its suggested retail price. If most of the people trying the product like it and are willing to buy it, that should be a good sign. If, however, the results are at all mixed, I would suggest that the prospective distributor find another company or at least another product.

Even a good product with a viable market must also be competitively and/or reasonably priced. If an item is overpriced, the distributor will be placed in the embarrassing position of having to defend the unrealistic pricing. This will make it hard to sell the product and even more difficult to sponsor new distributors.

An indirect indication of overpricing is often present when extravagant compensation claims are made. For example, beware when a would-be sponsor tells a prospective distributor that his or her company's compensation plan is much better than the competition's. Amway and Shaklee, for example, have refined both their manufacturing process and their compensation program so as to maximize the sales appeal of their products. Something is probably amiss when a new company, which does not duplicate the efficiency and research endeavors of Amway and Shaklee, boasts that it sells better products at lower prices and with greater compensation. Either the quality must go down or the price must go up to balance the higher compensation figures. The world's greatest compensation program is of little worth if the product is of poor quality or is extravagantly priced.

The prospective distributor must next be assured that there will be an adequate and consistent supply of the product to meet the potential needs of the distributor and the eventual "downline." Supply problems often arise in new multilevel businesses for two basic reasons. On the one hand, the logistics of keeping widespread distributors consistently supplied are fairly monumental. As orders are processed, there must be an efficient office and delivery system—something that normally takes some time to develop. On the other hand, when a company enjoys early sales success, it often reaches what has been termed "the flashpoint." This is the point in time when sales begin to grow in a geometric fashion. Since successful multilevel marketing businesses often grow geometrically, a new company often reaches a point where there are too many distributors putting too much demand on the company's production and delivery systems. When the company cannot meet its distributors' needs, the distributors are forced to wait for product. This creates a logjam for both sponsoring and selling.

If the company does not manufacture its own products, another problem often arises. If the company has difficulties with its suppliers, the bulk of its supply may be lost in the process.

It is obvious that maintaining an adequate and continuing supply of product is no simple task. It takes planning and expertise and often requires the development of regional offices and warehouses, linked with a main office by intricate computer and other communication systems. Amway and Shaklee have excelled in this area—they have both production and distribution capability and the know-how to maintain a continuing product flow. They also have the financial capacity to weather unforeseen difficulties.

Review of some points previously mentioned will help to illustrate how Amway and Shaklee have taken long strides in the direction of efficient product distribution. By devoting millions of square feet of building space to production, office, and warehouse functions on a regional, national, and international levels, these two companies have ensured a steady supply line between production and the consumer. For example, on the manufacturing side, Shaklee has taken steps to provide that much of its production can be increased as much as 300 percent without adding many new costs or increasing its manufacturing facilities. Amway has taken similar steps to keep up with its projected growth. On the delivery side, Amway has developed its own trucking fleet to keep products on the road, and Shaklee has relocated its distribution facilities to a more centrally located transportation hub. New companies without such planning capabilities are often unable to cope with supply difficulties.

Unfortunately, many distributors in new multilevel businesses try to circumvent potential supply problems by building large inventories. Some companies even improperly encourage inventory loading. In addition to representing a substantial investment, these inventories may prove to be a great liability if a product is taken off the market, if a product line is changed (as it often is in the early stages of a new business), or if the company itself folds. If a company falls on bad times, even its assurances that it will buy back inventory may be worthless. Obviously, if the company lacks the money to stay in operation, it will not have the money to buy back unused inventory.

2. Company Management.

Even after a prospective distributor has been satisfied that the business being considered meets all the above product criteria, he or she must be assured that the business is well-managed at all levels. Astute and capable corporate management is necessary to the success of any multilevel marketing business. Amway was founded by Rich DeVos and Jay Van Andel, two men who have served in numerous management and administrative capacities with startling success. Amway also has a number of professionally trained managers serving in major capacities throughout the business. For example, in addition to many management-level employees with advanced business degrees and training, Amway has a full staff of attorneys just to handle the legal tangles and regulatory matters that are inevitable in such an operation. Shaklee, which is now a public corporation, is strictly managed by professionals with extensive and impressive academic and corporate training and education. Even with professionally trained management, both Amway and Shaklee have been able to maintain the personal touch and an understanding of the needs of their distributors. DeVos and Van Andel have been distributors themselves; they know about all the potential problems and have taken every possible precaution to minimize them. Likewise, Gary Shansby of

Shaklee Corporation has developed a real feel for the needs of Shaklee's distributors, recognizing that they are the lifeblood of the business.

To be successful, a company must have management-level personnel with vision, understanding of the problems of a distributor, competence in administering a complex business, experience—and, most important of all, integrity. Many new companies simply do not have the resources to retain management personnel with all of these qualities, and the absence of any one can be fatal to the success of the business.

Many new businesses are long on vision and sell a beautiful "castle in the sky," but are short on the talents necessary to bring that castle down to earth so that it can be lived in. Dreams and vision are necessary ingredients in any successful multilevel business, but there must be something more, since a person will not long survive on dreams alone. In the words of a psychology professor I once had in college, "There is nothing wrong with building castles in the sky; it is just when we try to move into them permanently that we have problems." In multilevel marketing, there must be dreams, but they must be molded and formed by rationality, strategic planning, and professional management.

3. Compensation Plan.

Once the product and management criteria are met, it is time for a would-be distributor to examine the compensation plan in detail. To begin with, the program must reward production, not luck. Any person involved in the business should have the capability of passing anyone else in the business, based solely on productivity. There should be no special benefits for just being the first person involved, unless productivity is increased because of that person's effort and talent.

The compensation plan must also be reasonable. Many new companies boast that they have the most lucrative compensation plan on the market. Something is generally amiss when a company makes such claims. If a company implies that one can succeed without much effort or that one can make a phenomenal income in a very short period of time, the business is probably too good to be true. Running a successful multilevel distributorship is hard work. Although it can be enjoyable, growth rarely comes overnight. Companies that offer the type of extravagant claims that typically surround lotteries or sweepstakes generally have no more winners than do the lotteries and sweepstakes—and they have many, many losers.

The compensation plan of a reputable multilevel business will have a lucrative potential, but it should be free from such extravagant claims as: "The new distributor is really lucky to get in on the ground floor and will be able to make a fortune off the labor of those he or she gets involved below him." Such a representation implies that the "early bird" will be able to reap the reward of those who are silly enough to do all the work. Nevertheless, many companies use just such an appeal, and these companies should be avoided.

There is a third matter that should be of some concern. The compensation plan should be static. In other words, it should remain consistent, so that distributors will always know where they stand relative to the business. Many new businesses engage in repeated changes in their compensation program, to the dismay of their distributors. A company that has engaged in a number of such changes should be approached warily.

Amway and Shaklee both have plans that are consistent

with each of the points just raised. Their plans compensate those who produce, compensation figures do not change, and they avoid extravagant claims. With a solid multilevel business, the truth is always good enough. These companies acknowledge that not everyone succeeds, but many do. Thus, both Amway and Shaklee have been able to substantiate that year after year their respective compensation plans enable thousands of new distributors to rise to very successful levels. The greatest test of a company's compensation plan is whether it really works, not whether it looks good on paper.

4. Training and Sales Assistance.

A final criterion that must be met for a multilevel opportunity to be considered worthwhile is a sincere commitment by the company to provide quality sales and training programs. The prospective distributor should first examine the quality of the materials and the nature and extent of the "upline" support. The would-be distributor should look at whether the materials are of professional quality and whether they offer realistic and helpful advice. Both Amway and Shaklee have excellent sales and training aids which have been developed by professionals. These materials are filled with helpful advice based on actual experience and represent a refined sales and sponsorship process. The materials of any other multilevel opportunity ought to conform to those kinds of high standards.

In the sales and training area, a prospective distributor should take a hard look at the "upline," the immediate sponsor, and the accessible distributors above the sponsor. The line of sponsorship is important in a couple of related senses. First of all, if a new distributor has access to a sponsor who is really successful and who is willing to help develop a new distributor's business, the likelihood of success for that distributor is greatly enhanced. In an analogous sense, the early American explorers found the going very tough, but as they brought back information regarding the best routes, those who followed after them had an increasingly less difficult time. In this regard, the first successful distributors in a multilevel business have generally proceeded by trial and error, but with time and experience they have ultimately been able to pass along the best route to those they have sponsored.

The line of sponsorship is important in yet another sense. Beginning distributors who are really serious about being successful in their new business will find themselves in close and frequent contact with their "upline." A new distributor must be able to respect the veterans' abilities and experience, and must also believe that they are interested in his or her growth as a distributor and as a person. In short, a distributor and the "upline" must believe that their interests are compatible. If one gets involved with the wrong crowd, there may be guilt by association, but involvement with the right crowd can bring mutually beneficial *growth* by association.

A new distributor must respect his or her "upline" or line of sponsorship—because without their advice, a novice will have to blaze a new trail. Since every successful multilevel business has lines of sponsorship which are worthy of respect, it is senseless to ignore their invaluable advice in favor of striking out on one's own. Mutual trust between distributors on all levels is of prime importance, since it is the basis of compatibility.

Even in Amway and Shaklee, there are different types of sales organizations. There are groups with refined sales procedures, others that emphasize sponsorship, and still others that seek a balance of emphasis between the two related activities. The groups may differ only slightly, or sometimes fairly dramatically. Involvement should be with a sponsorship line which shares a new distributor's personalized aspirations in the business.

In selecting the "right" group one point should be emphasized. In no event should a sales group or organization encourage excessive purchases of their business aids. Such purchases should be kept to a minimum and should never exceed 20 percent of either the amount paid by a distributor for products or the gross business volume. These materials are useful tools for building product sales, but commissions are paid only on product sales to consumers. Furthermore, extensive sales of business tools may result in legal problems, since they may be viewed as indicative of an illegal pyramid activity. The reader will recall that one of the elements of an illegal pyramid is the sale of items not destined for consumption by the public. This problem is often compounded by the fact that such items are not returnable, particularly when sold by an independent sales organization rather than by the marketing organization itself. Therefore, this is an expense that cannot be recouped.

In regard to picking the right sales organization, some people have been unsuccessful in one or more multilevel endeavors, only to find that when they associated with the right group within a business, they have been able to build very successful distributorships. In fact, I recently read of an Amway distributor who had been involved in Amway on three different occasions. On the third occasion, when he associated with the right line of sponsorship and when his attitude was right, he rose to the Diamond level, which generally represents a gross annual income of between $75,000 and $150,000.

Therefore, I think that all would-be distributors must

look as closely at their "upline" as they do at the business itself. The sponsoring line will do much of the training on a day-to-day basis, and will also do the vast majority of encouraging and counseling. If choosing a multilevel business can be said to be analogous to plotting one's course in life, selecting an "upline" is a little like picking a spouse.

This brings me to a critical point with regard to Amway and Shaklee. (It is obvious that I am favorably impressed with both businesses.) Although there are a number of other successful multilevel-marketing organizations, Amway and Shaklee are proven performers. As a conservative lawyer, I prefer Amway and Shaklee for the same reason I would choose a McDonald's hamburger franchise over one for Jimmy's Burgers. McDonald's has the better track record and, all other things being equal, a McDonald's franchise is more likely to be successful. Jimmy's may be a great opportunity, but will require great patience as quirks are worked out of the marketing and production process. I would advise playing the percentages. It is clear that thousands of distributors in Amway and Shaklee will rise to new heights in their respective businesses each year. There is no similar assurance for many of the other multilevel businesses on the market today. Some will succeed; others will fail, while Amway and Shaklee can be expected to continue to grow at a rather regular rate.

I would not go so far as to recommend either Amway or Shaklee over the other one, since they both have similarities that have made them successful. They also have differences that may make one of them more appealing than the other. Therefore, I would recommend that an individual be sure that he/she is satisfied that one specific business best suits his or her needs, and that the chosen distributorship has a sponsoring line that can be fully trusted and respected.

Based on the results of a personal investigation into the four-point criteria mentioned above, a would-be distributor should be able to make a rational decision. That puts the responsibility for selecting the right business precisely where it should be—on the shoulders of the new distributor. That is a proper first step toward being responsible for one's own success or failure.

For the many distributors who will get involved in opportunities other than Amway or Shaklee, I should indicate that I believe many of you will be successful if the selected business meets the criteria set forth in this chapter. If you have carefully considered your choice and have prudently weighed all the factors involved, you should proceed with the attitude that you are involved in the best business on the market and should do all you can to make it so. Multilevel marketing of the right product under the right circumstances will be the ticket to economic independence for many people in the 1980s.

13

Some Concluding Remarks

In his recent book, *America in Search of Itself,* Theodore H. White noted that:

> In the 1950s, real income had gone up by 37 percent; in the 1960s, by 34 percent. But in the 1970s, growth of "real income" stalled. According to the AFL-CIO study, a real decrease began in the buying power of working men and women in 1977, and for the years since, though their wages go up, their take-home pay buys less and less. Late in 1981, the Census Bureau confirmed this morbid view of American working life in the year 1980: That year, said the Census, the real income of median families, after discounting for inflation, had dropped by 5.5 percent, the largest drop in real income since records had been kept.

With each drop in real income, a pervasive sense of economic helplessness gains new momentum in our country. Many Americans simply have lost faith in the American Dream—it is no longer believable for them. They want to believe, but their hope is dwindling.

Throughout the late seventies and early eighties, many people received raises, but the real value of those increases

165

in income has often failed to keep pace with inflation. Furthermore, with each jump in income there is the threat of entering a new and more costly income-tax bracket. The two factors have combined to produce a gradual decline in real income, as government, in effect, takes a larger bite of what is actually a smaller pie.

As mentioned in the first chapter, many Americans countered this "morbid" trend, to use Theodore White's terminology, by having both spouses work, whether or not this was their wish. Economic necessity simply forced many couples to seek a second job income. However, once the wife joined the husband in the marketplace (or vice versa), there was no potential worker left in the household who could go to work to counter future losses in real income. As buying power decreased, many families had no way to reverse the ill effects of the trend. Of course, some tried to work additional hours, although they once again found themselves up against tax bracketing problems. In many cases, with each extra hour worked, each additional dollar earned proportionately increased the overall bite that the government at all levels could take from their income. Furthermore, the extra hours away from home often placed an added burden on marital relationships, as well as imposing possible hardships on the family struc-ture. At some point, physical exhaustion from multiple jobs at overly long hours combined with continuing con-cern about effective income to bring complete economic frustration. The couple then begins to give up on their dreams—hoping merely to be able to continue to get by.

All of this gives rise to the major characteristic that I believe works in favor of legitimate marketing opportuni-ties. Genuine economic need plus the desire to better one's self equals what I call "need in search of a vehicle." Therefore, with need and desire working together, multilevel businesses are of great appeal to many would-be distributors when they see the whole picture. It can provide the means—in their spare time and often in husband-wife distributorships—to provide a very substantial second income from a business which can usually be run from a home base. In fact, particularly with the compensation features of such organizations as Amway and Shaklee, legitimate multilevel marketing can provide a second income that eventually exceeds the income received from a regular job.

The low down-side risk of multilevel marketing and its almost unbelievable up-side potential make it very appealing to many people who desire a better future for themselves and their families. For many Americans, there simply is no better way to add to real income on a consistent and developing basis.

While I have previously discussed the risk element of multilevel marketing in some depth, it would be well to summarize some of my conclusions at this juncture. On the one hand, multilevel marketing is a low-risk endeavor in an economic sense. Unlike many businesses, including a typical franchise with a proven track record, multilevel marketing should not involve the expenditure of large sums of money in its early stages.

Start-up costs are minimal, and the expenses of maintaining the business can and should be kept to a minimum as well.

On the other hand, multimarketing involves a substantial investment of time and effort, and also has a unique risk that is fairly common—perceived loss of status. The risk of time is straightforward. The money made in a multilevel business is based on one's personal production and that of one's sales organization. Both of these facets require effort. To build a sales group, one must contact others, show them the business, and then train and work with them in developing their own operations. This typically takes a large amount of time and effort. Additionally, products must be demonstrated or explained, and this also takes time.

Although this time expenditure can be allocated on a part-time basis, often before or after regular working hours, building a substantial multilevel business does require in the neighborhood of approximately twenty hours per week for most growing distributorships. Wise time management can somewhat ease the pressure, but no success comes without toil and sacrifice. There can be substantial rewards, but they do not come easily. This, of course, is true of virtually all business ventures.

Perceived loss of status is a less common risk in other types of business activity. This is the risk faced when staking one's dreams on the marketing of soap, vitamins, or similar mundane though necessary products, rather than aspiring to be president of a bank or some other large status-generating concern. Most people would be proud to be president of Proctor & Gamble, a major soap producer, although they would not be as honored to be labeled a soap salesperson. Unfortunately, there is not much room at the highest levels of the Proctor & Gamble executive hierarchy—but there is a great deal of room for high achievement in legitimate multilevel businesses. This is particularly true of people who are willing to put the potential for success ahead of the notion that there is more stature in being at the top of some corporate pyramid.

Most Americans who have the desire to find a vehicle to meet their economic needs are quickly able to put any status objections behind them. They can recognize that there is little chance that they will reach the top of their own particular professional hierarchy. They also come to realize that the types of products dealt with in the multilevel context are important because they facilitate repeat sales, month after month, thereby creating a formidable business foundation. Finally, they recognize that the practical virtues of the products outweigh any status considerations. Many distributors not only overcome their initial status objections, but later become solid advocates of their product lines, as they learn of their quality and performance.

The new distributor learns that growth in a multilevel business is like building a multistory high-rise. One begins with a solid foundation and then, floor by floor, adds the remainder of the structure, using quality products and proven building techniques. In many other types of business, what is built one day must be rebuilt or repeated the next day. For example, as a teacher, I must teach a class day after day to receive my paycheck. My prior labor may result in promotion, but the fact remains that I must do the same job over and over again. In the law-school context, after three years, we hope that we have adequately trained a group of law students, and new students will take their places. I am forever building the first floor, without continuing income residuals or overrides. Not so in the multilevel marketing business, where one can build a formidable organization and can work at refining it in the future.

This raises another point. In a multilevel business, one actually receives increased compensation in the future for what is done today. Month after month, a distributor is compensated for the strength of the structure he or she has built in the past. The future is always brighter than yesterday or today, since past performance pays dividends tomorrow.

To build an ongoing profitable distributorship, one must help others to be successful, by training them in all aspects of the business. The trainees, in turn, are able to help build on what they have learned. The key to building a secure multilevel sales organization is a desire and ability to help others build a profitable business for themselves and their "downline."

If a distributor relates well with the "upline" in learning the business, and with the "downline" in teaching the business, he or she can reap more than monetary success. Distributors can build lasting friendships and have fun in the process. In fact, I have friends in multilevel marketing who stress that they would be involved even if there was no money to be made—just for the friendships they have built and for the personal development they have experienced. Frankly, I do not know how sincere they are in making such a statement, but I do know that they gain satisfaction from their businesses that often transcends dollars and cents.

It should be obvious that I sincerely believe in the potential of multilevel marketing and its roots in the free-enterprise concept of payment for one's productivity, regardless of race, religion, or national origin. It should also be clear that I recognize that not all succeed, and that multilevel marketing is not for everyone, since it is a challenge that some people are not prepared to accept.

It is not for those who do not have the time or the inclination to concentrate on building the business. It is also not for those who do not enjoy working with and helping other people toward success. Finally, multilevel marketing is generally not for people who do not really need the extra income.

Objections concerning possible market saturation and pyramiding are largely unfounded. There is adequate opportunity for all, even starting at the ground-floor level. I have previously shown that saturation and the pyramid objections pose no realistic threat to legitimate multilevel marketing operations. In fact, there is probably no better time than now for associating with a reputable multilevel business. Both the products and the business methods are forever improving, and multilevel marketing continues to grow at phenomenal rates, year after year.

Therefore, if one cannot legitimately claim a lack of time or a lack of desire to work with other people or a lack of need for more income, he or she has few objections to getting involved in a multilevel business. Even assertions that one lacks the necessary ability are unsupported, because sponsors train their "downline," and are probably more qualified to make initial decisions regarding one's abilities.

If, as a would-be distributor, or even as an active but not really committed distributor, you still have some un-founded reservations or objections, I believe some counsel I received from my daughter when she was just three years old may be of some benefit to you.

One evening, I was upset with my daughter, Mary, so I told her to go up to her room. I was very emphatic and demanded that she go upstairs immediately, and I did not want any "ifs, ands, or buts about it." After hearing my command, she looked up into my eyes, with that look of innocent dismay that normally can be found only on the face of a young child, and said, "Oh, Daddy, don't you know that 'but' is a bathroom word?"

I chuckled at the time, believing that I had heard something cute. However, later I reflected on what Mary had said. She was right. "But"—as we generally use it—*is* a bathroom word. We use it to rationalize why we have not done something that we know we could and should do. For example, when my mother becomes offended at my failure to write her as often as I should, I generally rationalize my failure with a statement like "Mom, I love you and I know that I should write, *but*. . . ."

If you are on the verge of getting involved in multilevel marketing and have examined the business aspects of such an opportunity in the detail suggested throughout this book, I would recommend that you give it a try, unless you have come up with a bona fide objection. If you do not have a legitimate excuse, you should remember that "but" is often a word that stands in the way of genuine growth opportunities, at both the personal and economic levels. The risks are low and the potential is high. It is worth a real try, particularly if you follow the suggestions outlined in this book.

Writing this book has been work, but it has also been fun. In fact, it has been a lot like being involved in a multilevel business. I agree with Rich DeVos—life is exciting, if we only have the faith and desire necessary to make it so.